ROAR

HOW TO STAND UP FOR YOUR LIFE'S TRUE PURPOSE

DANIEL HABIF

Translated by Cecilia Molinari

**PRIMERO
SUEÑO PRESS**

ATRIA

New York London Toronto Sydney New Delhi

PRIMERO
SUEÑO PRESS

ATRIA

An Imprint of Simon & Schuster, LLC
1230 Avenue of the Americas
New York, NY 10020

This publication contains the opinions and ideas of its author. It is intended to provide helpful and informative material on the subjects addressed. It is sold with the understanding that the author and publisher are not engaged in rendering medical, health or other personal or professional services in the book.

This Primero Sueño Press/Atria Paperback edition September 2024

PRIMERO SUEÑO / **ATRIA** PAPERBACK and colophon are trademarks of Simon & Schuster, LLC

Simon & Schuster: Celebrating 100 Years of Publishing in 2024

For information about special discounts for bulk purchases, please contact Simon & Schuster Special Sales at 1-866-506-1949 or business@simonandschuster.com.

The Simon & Schuster Speakers Bureau can bring authors to your live event. For more information or to book an event, contact the Simon & Schuster Speakers Bureau at 1-866-248-3049 or visit our website at www.simonspeakers.com.

Interior design by Joy O'Meara

Manufactured in the United States of America

1 3 5 7 9 10 8 6 4 2

Library of Congress Cataloging-in-Publication Data has been applied for.

ISBN 978-1-6680-5684-4
ISBN 978-1-6680-5685-1 (ebook)

I will remain at the edge of this book
until I see you roar.

Roar

is a book

that will

highlight

you.

Before you reign, you will eat dust, you will be sold out by your friends and relatives. You cannot fly with those who clip your wings, so stop sighing and start progressing, for dreams aren't made of laziness or apathy.

Your glory will be seen as a failure by the mediocre, who will forgive anything but your success. Since happiness doesn't tolerate cowardice, you will never see an impassive person make history. If you tenaciously persevere, you will remember the safe places of your childhood, and you will behold the most intense, powerful gaze you will ever see: your own.

Even when everything seems pointless, never give up. Let the impossible be your plaything. Instead of waiting for destiny, you must seize it.

Roar
or expect to be devoured.

Contents

CONTENTS

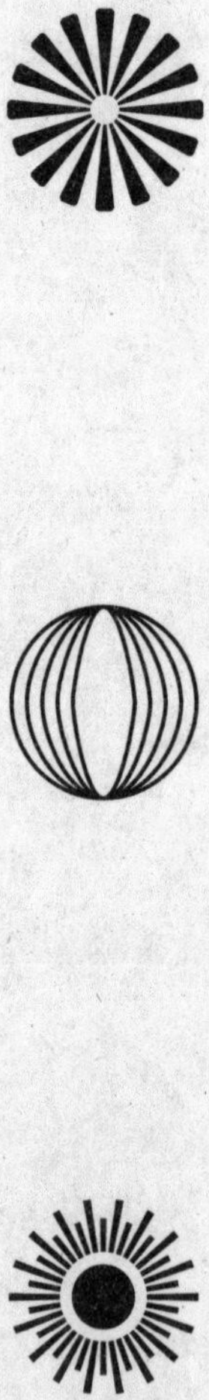

Introduction

We live in a world that changes at breakneck speed. Competition is fierce and time waits for no one. But what if you feel like you just can't keep up? What if you just don't have the strength to fight for your place in the world? The universe's response is swift and brutal: Stand up for your purpose or run the risk of being devoured. After the pandemic, that very message slapped me in the face. I felt the world was closing in on me, domesticating me. I felt my soul withering away and my strength and purpose slipping through my fingers. I had a pent-up scream clawing at my stifled throat, gagged by the oppressive censorship that I had imposed on it, silencing my dreams.

But as hopeless as things seemed, my soul's message overcame my doubts. It demanded that I stop whispering. My soul told me it was time to shout. To release ourselves from the confines of our doubts and fears, demolish the walls and bend the bars that have been holding us back, we need to find the courage to take responsibility for our actions and decisions. We need to take initiative in the face of intimidating challenges. We need to take risks that aren't always perfectly calculated and be okay if the results aren't what we expected. Ultimately, we need to find the courage to Roar.

NO MORE SILENCE.

INTRODUCTION

Roar is a manifesto for those who refuse to be victims of circumstance, for those who choose to roar with strength and claim their place in the world. This book is the result of keen observation and a profound understanding of modern society's relentless nature. It represents our indomitable energy, the fierce determination that drives us to face our fears, to push our limits, and to fight for our dreams with courage and passion.

In these pages you will find three seemingly simple steps—inhale, inflame, and roar—filled with the tools and techniques you need to face adversity, embrace your purpose, become an effective leader, influence others positively, make decisions that benefit both you and your community, and emerge stronger and more determined than ever. Assuming leadership roles and exercising authority are acts of courage and conviction. It may all sound pretty simple, but the path of self-discovery is an internal battle with yourself. It requires a committed effort, the kind you must make within you.

As you take each of these three steps, you will begin to see your greatness unfold and your purest essence reveal itself. You will also wrestle with this question: Is it possible to bend without breaking in life? Figuring out when to be flexible and when to stand strong in your power will be essential as you face the relentless challenges on your journey. We've been raised to believe that strength and rigidity are symbols of power, resistance, and determination. And there will most definitely be moments in our lives when we will need this strength to overcome obstacles. Yet flexibility is an equally powerful quality because it allows us to adapt to changing circumstances in an ever-evolving world and navigate the storms of life without breaking.

Lao Tzu once said, "Water is fluid, soft, and yielding. But water will wear away the rock, which is rigid and cannot yield.... This is

2

another paradox: what is soft is strong." Those who are rigid and resistant to change may find themselves worn down by circumstances. Are you overdoing it? Is it time to be more flexible and less unyielding? I'm not asking you to abandon your strength or set aside your convictions and simply go with the flow. Sometimes we need to be the strong and rigid rock to stay on our feet. But other times it's best to be like water, navigating around obstacles and finding our way through narrow paths despite the barriers before us. This is the dichotomy between endurance and adaptability, rigor and fluidity. To roar we must recognize that sometimes true strength lies in the ability to bend without breaking.

The time has come to raise your voice, plunge into the storm with a boldness that does not fear failure, and emerge with scars that make you proud, for risk and failure are some of our wisest teachers. Join me as we challenge our self-imposed limits, break free from the chains of conformity, and dare to be different in a world that celebrates similarity. The greatest risk is to risk nothing at all.

FAILURE IS A THOUSAND TIMES BRAVER THAN NOT TRYING.

 INHALE ————————————————

Inhaling is the energetic charge that provides the opportunity for a profound revision of our beliefs and behaviors. It involves filling ourselves with the healing air of stillness. It defines us. In any attempt at a new beginning, we must first examine the pillars that support us. We must audit the flows of our emotional balance sheet to stop the transactions that bleed us dry and close the accounts with creditors who demand payments for bills we no longer owe. The fiercest debt collector is within us, with past-due statements of hurt and guilt. This accounting also records the wounds we have accumulated since our early childhood, and sums up our talents, values, convictions, and confidence, leading to a positive balance. We need to allow ourselves to evaluate our behaviors and tendencies, not to define who we are, but to have a starting point for our inner journey. Self-exploration is an urgent breath of fresh air when we have yet to emerge from the suffocation of everyday life.

First and foremost, we must confirm we are in a safe place. If we want our cries to be heard, we must find security and stability for our current murmurs. Who can we confide in about the shame caused by our shortcomings? Who can we fearlessly be ourselves with? That is what we need to determine to feel safe on this journey.

Self-exploration is accompanied by our environment, in other words, what we have chosen to include in our personal kingdom, such as money, relationships, and business. We grant these elements a power that is clearly manifested in our interactions with them, and the hierarchy and weight we give them modify certain conditions in our lives. Self-evaluation reveals who we honor: from the people we love or admire to the institutions, symbols, concepts, or ideologies we respect. This shapes our ideals. Honor exposes and largely tells us who we are and what defines us.

Of course, there is no way to fill ourselves if we remain empty of God. Even nonbelievers should find a connection within themselves between their physical reality and that dimension of mystery, which somehow is obsessively described by hundreds of theories, even though none allows us to fully understand it. Each new discovery related to the elementary aspects of physics brings us closer to God and moves us away from a mechanical understanding of the universe. The act of inhalation is therefore an appropriate time to quietly reflect on death itself and to remember our ability to conceive life.

In short, to inhale is to empty ourselves of ourselves and fill up with the eternal, with the imperishable, with the fabulous mystery that makes us who we are. In that mystery is where we will redis-cover ourselves by asking the questions we know how to answer but find so hard to articulate. And that will prepare us to finally release the explosion within us.

 ## INFLAME

Once we have filled our chest, we need to inflame it, gather those reflections of who we are, and create an action plan. To do this, we must first learn the most important skill: how to make intelligent decisions. This involves looking ahead without being obscured by the biases and fallacies that make up our mental models. There is no such thing as a perfect decision; you would only come to one by chance. Our job is to know the root causes of the distortions that repeatedly lead us to make the same mistakes.

> LOVE IS NOT A MIRACLE, IT'S A DECISION;
> AND THE MIRACLE **IS TO**
> **MAKE THAT DECISION EVERY DAY.**

Then, we will traverse the storms of hatred and criticism that try to tear us away from who we are until we are stripped of the strength to move forward. Crossing them, even when we know we may be shipwrecked, will help replenish us and help us reach the calm and clear skies of trust and peace. We will review the opinions we receive and the reasons behind our reactions to them. If we ran a hundred-meter dash with our eyes locked on the crowd instead of the path ahead of us, we wouldn't find our way to the finish line. Paying attention to those judgmental eyes forces us to lose our focus on succeeding. Just because some people come to a standstill to fixate on us doesn't mean we should stop too.

Next, we'll examine what we're focusing on. Awareness is a talent that needs to be refined. Concentrating our entire attention on the present is a luxury that not everyone can afford in a world hung up on urgencies. Yet to move forward we must devote all our attention to our path and avoid getting caught up in resentment, guilt, or the past. Before we roar, we must hold our breath and concentrate on what we want to do and how we will achieve it.

At a time when the noise around us is never silent, being able to focus on what's right for us is one of our greatest virtues. Noise reaches us even in moments of rest. Pressing pause has gone from a fertilizer to a pollutant in our imagination. Resting is no longer an opportunity to be authentic, but an incentive to become a crude imitation of others.

To inflame also means to learn how to identify who has tied strings over our shoulders to manipulate us like puppets. Being aware of what influences us takes on transcendent weight in times when we have lost control of what we consume. Information overload, which our parents and grandparents were able to control to some degree, has become immeasurably powerful in our lives.

This situation actually raises the value of knowing how we can influence others. We've been taught that persuasion is a method that makes others comply with our will, even if they don't want to. But that doesn't work. We have been mistakenly looking for a magic lamp to fulfill our desire for mental control, when the right path is to understand how our ideas, with their strengths and weaknesses, are most conveniently and adequately examined.

IT'S NICE TO WAKE UP AND SEE THE REFLECTION OF **A GOOD PERSON**.

Persuasion is just a way of emphasizing your perspectives, making them heard, and getting your peers to feel comfortable with them, even if your vision doesn't align with theirs. Getting people to do what you want, at whatever cost, means moving away from influence and into the dark realms of manipulation. That's why we've devoted a section to techniques that will help us have a positive effect on others while we also learn to defend ourselves against manipulative schemes.

To turn the air's stillness into a roar we need will power. In this step, we'll be talking about this key tool, and we'll dive into the struggle that takes place between two people living at different points in time: those who enjoy immediate pleasure and those who look to the future, with whom we don't always identify. At this crossroads, we must choose between a short road to a guaranteed pleasure and a long and unpredictable one that will lead us to the destination of our dreams.

 ROAR

This last step deals with the roar's power, with facts, actions, and their meaning. It's a beginning, a gamble that we can't take back, where we must place a bet on the person we wish to become. And it all starts with self-control.

Understanding the importance of self-control will allow us to sophisticatedly navigate through time, choosing either to stay in the fleeting pleasure of the present or to focus on a prosperous future. The latter will be possible if we know how to invest in our ideals, desires, emotions, and behaviors. Every effort, every endeavor, every sacrifice increases the balance of our expected benefit.

To get there, we must trade silence for inner peace. Many times we remain silent because it's an easy way out, but instead of lifting some of the weight off our shoulders, we only end up stockpiling even more anxieties, which continue to grow incessantly. Sometimes we stay silent to escape reality, and other times, even worse, we do it to let others deal with what we can't face.

Surprisingly, one of the key steps to inflaming our confined power is abandonment: letting go of some learned things that we hold to be absolute truths. It can be strangely easy to stop doing things we like, but letting go of things that hurt us can be a real struggle. We want to be strong, but we don't realize that it takes more strength to be vulnerable than to be brutal, because vulnerability is a way of being unbreakable. Learning to let go is a badge of courage and integrity: It's brave to assume the consequences; it's honorable to assume our responsibility.

YOU PRAY FOR GOD TO REMOVE YOUR BURDENS, **BUT YOU CLING TO THEM**.

This discussion questions how many mistakes we're willing to process and how to make them work in our favor. We have borrowed the term *resilience* from materials science and applied it to describe our behavior. The results I've seen lead me to one of two possible conclusions: that we still have a lot to learn about engineering, or

WHEN YOU OPEN
A BOOK,

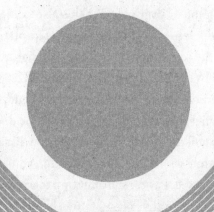

A PAIR
OF WINGS
APPEARS.

that we still don't know how to decipher human behavior. We insist on confusing resilience with resistance, on giving the former the attributes of the latter, and neither gains value.

The more pressure you contain, the more you increase the power and volume of your roar. Yet this also comes with greater exhaustion, which makes succumbing to temptation and being swept away by the comfort of a liberatingly soft sigh quite a seductive option. Take a breath, hold it in your chest, and let out a powerful scream that empties the silences contained in your pains and fears. That's what it means to roar: to ride wildly in the direction of your dreams. Some will call it a dust cloud; others will say it's a trick, a circus; but blasting what you hold dear within you is instrumental.

Listen to yourself. Pay careful attention to what you have to say to yourself. Ignore the attacks and taunts before they muffle your voice. Determine exactly what the tone and boldness of your cry will be. And unleash that pent-up power.

Make them tremble.

Roar! May everyone hear what you have to say.

Roar! May you have nothing left inside.

Roar! May you end the tyranny of silence.

Step One

INHALE

In the prelude to great moments in your life, you prepared yourself for action. Remember? You stopped and expanded your chest with a breath that cleansed the fears embedded within you. That's what happened seconds before you brushed across those lips: You paused to take in a long breath before attempting that kiss; you closed your eyes and expanded as if in a ritual encapsulating your fears.

The times you dared to pedal without help were wonderful, the first time you swam deep into the sea, the time you crossed the dark alley of so many nightmares alone. It happened just before the great moments—that inhalation announced you would say yes, you would initiate that change, you would finally decide to let go of the pain you were carrying. You inhaled to prepare yourself, and after you exhaled, you took the step that had been so hard to take.

Unfortunately, with the arrival of obligations to fulfill and bills to pay, the impulse that drove you to move forward with your dreams weakened. You began to distance yourself from what you wanted, passions disappeared, and suddenly you stopped recognizing yourself in the mirror. Audacious inspiration ceased to appear with the same frequency; your heart became constricted; your soul went silent; and the muffled roar in your throat began to wither.

To regain that breath you need to relearn how to fill your chest, to swell with courage, and this begins with the act of knowing yourself in depth. It is time to take back what belongs to you, to set aside time to talk with yourself, and to do so regarding who you are. We have spent a good part of our lives learning about numbers and doctrines, about the names of trees and literary devices, about the erosion of rocks and the heroes who wrote our past, but far less time has been taken to teach us how to get to know ourselves: to understand how we think or why we think the way we do.

Gathering the momentum to roar involves rediscovering ourselves, knowing our attachments, identifying our talents, and understanding why we carry wounds that condition our behaviors.

In the following pages, I will guide you through this process. It all begins with a deep breath that you can turn into a tornado.

THE BODY DANCES WITH ANYBODY,
**BUT THE SOUL DOES NOT LAUGH
WITH ANYONE.**

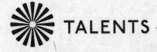 ## TALENTS

One of the reasons we are unable to pursue the activities we most enjoy is the burden of wondering if we have the right talents. Many people are unaware of their true skills, and they will never get to discover them if they remain where they never have the opportunity to put them into practice. This may be your case. We've been conditioned to ignore our talents because we're still tied to an educational system that seems sometimes not only to hide them, but also to stifle their development. How can we know our talents if we've spent our lives surrounded by obstacles that prevent us from using them?

THE COMFORT ZONE IS ALSO
A CONFLICT ZONE.

First, we've been led to believe that ability and talent are one and the same. But we need to differentiate them. Talent is natural, one of the many gifts God brings us into the world with. Everyone, without exception, has multiple talents—we have innate aptitudes in intellectual, physical, emotional, and even spiritual areas—but not everyone enjoys them. On the other hand, ability is something that can be learned, even if it is extremely complicated.

Music is the most common example used to explain this difference. We all know someone with great musical talent: They are effortlessly in tune, have rhythm and an amazing ability to pick up and repeat melodies. However, these people could not play an instrument without having studied and practiced it. On the other hand, someone without these gifts but with an unwavering sense of discipline could develop the ability to play an instrument and interpret a piece by Mozart or Chopin to perfection. But this would only be possible after a colossal effort—it wouldn't come as naturally to them. The same can happen in other fields.

No untapped talent can surpass the skills of discipline, but no discipline can produce the passion that comes from expressing raw talent. The great leaders in various fields have achieved mastery through a combination of natural talent, aptitude, perseverance, and effort. That's why it's important to identify your natural talents if you don't already know them.

I am no longer surprised when a friend or family member says they don't know what their talent is, but I still find it alarming that there are so many people who blatantly say they have no talent. This is what we have been taught to think. Everyone has a talent. The best recipe for discovering it is to venture out and try something you've never done before, no matter how simple it may seem, while genuinely believing that you will find a talent within you in these attempts.

If we explore our options by first defining what we are not, it's difficult for our natural abilities to manifest themselves. In other words, if we have preconceived notions about what we are capable of doing, we will get very different results. From a young age, maybe you were taught to say, "I suck at sports," because your parents didn't sign you up for activities you liked; they put you in the ones they liked. Since you didn't make it into the top three of those events, they hung the "terrible at sports" medal on you, and you accepted it. So you've lived all these years believing that because you're not good at something, you're bad at everything. You won't be able to find your gifts if you only look in those dark corners of your life.

You must find your hidden talent, and as Luke states in 15:8–9: "Or what woman having ten pieces of silver, if she loses one piece, doth not light a lamp, and sweep the house, and seek diligently until she finds it? And when she hath found it, she calleth together her friends and neighbors, saying, 'Rejoice with me for I have found the piece which I had lost.'" First, she turns on the light (how do we turn on the light of our mind?) to see clearly. Next, she uses the broom to sweep the places that are most difficult for her to clean, and then she is ready to search with extreme care. She is never indifferent to what is lost or hidden; on the contrary, she is extremely diligent and, above all, she wants to find the coin with great fervor.

Your talent is a treasure to be sought. Many do not search for their talent because they don't think it's a valuable treasure worth the effort. They compare the amount of effort to the returns they think they'll get from a talent they've minimized because they've miscalculated its value. Do not underestimate the size of that treasure, for it may be the weapon that will lead to your victory. There are no small talents.

Skills are given to you by someone else. For example, you can learn pastry-making from the best teachers, but what you feel when you bake your first cake is something that only belongs to you. If you haven't found your talent yet, I bet it's hiding in the activities you think you're bad at. Remember, don't look for it in the outcome but in what you feel when you do it.

OUR GREATEST CHALLENGE IN A MACHINE-FILLED WORLD
WILL BE TO ACT HUMANELY.

Talents are competitions that are easy for us, and we naturally find great pleasure in doing them. We are born with that ease, but we still have to work at developing them. Our ability to assimilate knowledge is conditioned by our thoughts. There are two opposing mindsets when we enter learning processes:

- **The fixed mindset:** found in those who believe that their skills do not change.

- **The growth mindset:** found in those who believe that any skill can be mastered through study and practice.

When a person with a fixed mindset says, "I don't know how to dance," they are describing a situation that they already consider to be set in stone. When someone with a growth mindset says, "I don't know how to dance," they are referring to the fact that they have not yet explored the resources to learn how to do it. This comes from the science of teaching and is good to remember at this point, because if you are dominated by a fixed mindset, you will not have the necessary stimuli to explore your talents.

In short, forget about everything you've been told and have believed you can and can't do. Forget about what you think you're failing at and start over. A good way to explore your talents is to pay attention to the people you admire, the ones who, when you see them developing their art, inspire you to say, "What would that feel like?" If you're on the right track, you'll be more moved by what these people experience at work than by the prestige or income they earn.

Another important step is to create a space for yourself in your everyday life to explore your talents. If routine and monotony take over, you won't find opportunities to try. Also, step away from the herd. When we insist on sticking to what others like, we limit our contact with the things we might like. This can happen without us even realizing it; going with the tide is a way of giving up who we can become.

Discovering your talents or reconciling with them is essential to roaring. They're the driving force you need to fill the void of silence.

 ## YOUR INTELLIGENCES ———————

As previously mentioned, discovering a talent implies learning, and this doesn't happen within the comfort of what we already know. It must be an adventure, and like explorers in a new field in nature, beyond the weeds we may find a meadow or rocky terrain, and we need to have the same willingness to cross them both. Learning something new involves the risk of stumbling, especially if we don't modify the way we walk.

Changing how we face ourselves is crucial. This isn't a minor detail; it's the key to the vault. We are observers, seekers, and permanent witnesses of our entire being, but we get lost within ourselves because we don't travel there often. Let's enter, cleanse, and conquer the breadth of our domain, leaving no land unexplored. Inside we will find a cosmos, a mirror of other universes and worlds. Let's tear down the shrines and caves we've used as a refuge to hide from ourselves. Let's confront ourselves so that we don't abandon ourselves. Let's visit, stay, and enjoy ourselves. Let's pick up the pieces that others have left behind, clean up, make room for ourselves, and stay there.

SOME ANSWERS ARE FOUND
IN THE DETAILS.

It's normal to think that we prefer to learn in a certain way. We've been taught as much for a long time. And yes, it's true that some techniques work better for some people than others, but that's not always the case, even if we study endlessly. Just as we must be open to new knowledge, we must also be open to using different ways of learning. We risk turning away from specific topics because we insist on adhering to the idea that "this is how I understand." That is a limiting belief we must abandon when we wish to discover inherent, unexplored talents.

Theories of learning styles have been popular for several decades. They're understood as the result of studying people's preferred mechanisms for digesting, translating, organizing, and interpreting new information. Knowing these preferences has helped us confirm the value of different instructional pathways. Thanks to these theories, many educators and students have adjusted their methods—the greatest contribution has been proving that not everyone should be treated equally when it comes to learning. But their usefulness ends when, instead of helping us grow, they limit us, because we think that if we have one optimal learning style, we don't need to explore the rest. We get rusty.

Forty years ago the psychologist Howard Gardner came up with the Theory of Multiple Intelligences, which he classified according to the type of information people use when processing a subject.[1] Initially, Gardner mentioned five types of intelligences, although his theory has given rise to the identification of many others. Most texts recognize eight.

The intelligences are presented as different programs that operate in our brain, with a fair number doing so independently. Some of these programs are more efficient than others. The greatest intelligences would be those with the most efficient algorithms in their software. This theory broke with a long-held view that intelligence was a unit that predicted efficient results across the board, regardless of the subject matter.

This approach demonstrates that a person may have a certain ease in some subjects, while not getting notable results in others. For example, one of the intelligences mentioned by Gardner is linguistic

WHEN YOU DON'T KNOW WHERE TO TURN, GO WITHIN.

intelligence, which processes information related to the meaning of words in various forms. People with a high linguistic ability are usually labeled as "intelligent," even if their spatial or mathematical processing is not particularly sharp. In other words, we usually perceive a person as intelligent when they express themselves with fluency and grace, even if they can't solve basic logistical problems or, even worse, the most common personal conflicts.

This "programming" observed by experts is associated with how the brain functions. For example, linguistic intelligence is related to the left temporal lobe and left frontal lobe, which are the areas connected to language comprehension and word formation (Wernicke's area and Broca's area). On the other hand, spatial intelligence is associated with the posterior regions of the right hemisphere, which are connected to visual ability.

MANY ASK QUESTIONS FOR THE SAKE OF BEING SEEN, NOT FOR THE SAKE OF LEARNING.

Perhaps you've insisted on pursuing talents that aren't in your most developed dimension, so I want to give you a brief description of the traits and contributions of the eight intelligences accepted by Gardner and most experts that followed him. This will help you understand what they represent and identify which ones prevail in you.

MUSICAL INTELLIGENCE

It includes elements that increase the potential to identify sounds, listen, sing, and play instruments. As a language, it helps to understand when a composition has some imbalance and allows one to interpret and create sound pieces. It's not only useful for musicians but also for the people who support them, such as music engineers, manufacturers, or sound programmers.

BODILY-KINESTHETIC INTELLIGENCE ————

It involves body control, both in simple expressions, as well as in hand-eye coordination and dexterity in fine and gross movements. This control supports the expression of ideas through movement and leads one to perform activities that require balance, coordination, and ease. It's necessary for athletes, actors, lecturers, dancers, or people who require outstanding motor skills, such as surgeons, metalsmiths, or carpenters.

LOGICAL-MATHEMATICAL INTELLIGENCE ————

It allows one to calculate, quantify, analyze, estimate results, and solve equations, as well as interpret numerical representations. It helps formulate quantitative statements and generate hypotheses. With it, patterns are identified and abstractions are made. It's exceptionally valuable in business, engineering, exact sciences, and computing.

SPATIAL INTELLIGENCE ————————

It helps to perceive the spatial world, not only on a large scale. Someone with this intelligence can imagine how movements in a field will take place, and it allows them to consider different scales. It also makes it easy to present visual ideas and concepts, sketch structures, and estimate distances. It's fundamental in the world of arts and communications, as well as in graphic, industrial, and civil works design.

LINGUISTIC INTELLIGENCE ———————————

It opens the door to formulating ideas using words—verbal or written—while accelerating the decoding of what others are expressing. It increases efficiency in speaking, writing, and appreciating messages. This skill is valued for its range, since it's useful in the arts, sales, leadership, and communication.

NATURALIST INTELLIGENCE ———————————

Although not last on this list, it was added by Gardner more than a decade after he came up with the other intelligences. It involves the understanding of the vastness of nature, processing information that allows one to identify and stratify environmental elements. To those who don't think this is a relevant dimension, I invite you to see how important it was to the development of our species in ancient times. It's fundamental for scientists, geologists, agricultural technicians, and artists.

INTERPERSONAL INTELLIGENCE ———————————

Considered a type of social awareness, it's the program we use to pick up on signals other people send about their intentions, emotions, tastes, and motivations. It allows us to interpret what others want and establish a connection with them. With this intelligence, we reinforce empathy and acknowledgment. It's essential for making group activities work, organizing leadership, and communicating in specific situations of affection, displeasure, or concern. While every area of human endeavor needs this intelligence, it's especially important for people whose jobs require interaction with others, such as leaders, educators, therapists, and customer service teams.

INTRAPERSONAL INTELLIGENCE

I chose to list this one last because I want you to pay special attention to it. This intelligence consists of the ability to access and interpret inner emotions, sensations, and feelings. We can use it to take an X-ray and see the factors that define us, such as our biases and judgments. This understanding helps us to distinguish between what's happening and what's causing us pain and discomfort, and it gives us a visual of how we'll react. Although it's extremely useful to anyone, it's of greatest value to people who need emotional control, who must maintain high-level relationships, or who have critical responsibilities.

We all have certain abilities in each of the intelligences. The strengths in one do not determine how the others play out within us: you can be a brilliant mathematician with minimal interpersonal skills, or a skilled mechanic with good communication skills. Although we have been taught otherwise, and partly because the educational system only recognizes and values some of them, intelligences are not always reflected in our grades, but they are intimately linked to what differentiates us from others. If you search online for "multiple intelligences quiz," you will find a wide variety of sites offering assessments to help you discover your predominant intelligences. Learning your predominant intelligences is a valuable exercise that can provide you with countless insights.

WASTE NO TIME WITH ME; IT'S USELESS TO TELL FIRE NOT TO BURN.

Although they stem from the study of similar fields, learning styles should not be confused with multiple intelligences. The former describes how we prefer to receive information; the latter, how we process it.

WILLINGNESS AND CONFIDENCE

Accumulating talents is of little use if it's not accompanied by the additional step that takes us from the good to the exceptional, from the admirable to the sublime. We often convince ourselves that we've done enough or that we've given our all to a specific situation. But deep down we know the raw truth is that we haven't given everything, and we're reminded of this by a voice that haunts and torments us. That voice must be heard, not silenced, because it's the voice of excellence, the one that raises your standards and pushes you to break free from the systematic comfort of everyday life and the often-used phrase: "I'm fine like this."

That voice echoes the roar of willingness and confidence. Willingness is an act of surrender, an act of commitment that prompts us to examine the motivators in our lives. What moves you: a dream, an addiction, a void, a man, a woman, money . . . ? Think about it. Willingness isn't easy, but it's a mandatory condition for excelling in any endeavor or dream.

We all have certain resources, and regardless of what we can count on, we work, study, move, and live. Yet it's interesting to see

DO YOU SEE THIS SCAR?

I GOT IT BECAUSE
I DIDN'T ADJUST
MY EXPECTATIONS.

how readily a person can list the resources they lack and how challenging it is for them to recognize the ones they have from birth.

The fundamental key is that it's not about the amount of talent, but the mindset that guides it. If you have the beautiful and significant virtue of willingness, I can assure you that your talents will multiply in strength, power, and reach. Respect yourself. Focus your will on going the extra mile. Increase your willingness and you will start to see blessings pouring into your life like a torrential rain.

Confidence is a fundamental part of willingness. It's the virtue of showing composure and optimism in any circumstance. Confidence often stems from the love you profess for a cause or an ideal. It has the luxury of being selective, but real leadership always demands it, because firm confidence, despite your staggering walk, doesn't let you give up. It's an ability that makes you an effective person in most situations.

Confidence is developed through extreme circumstances. No one builds their confidence without taking jittery, frightening steps. It is also a result of steadfastness and faith. Confidence is expressed through your hands, face, chest, attitude, and above all, through the energy you radiate when you speak. It provides sound judgment and vision. It modifies the energy of a place or a situation. If you don't believe in what you say, no one else will, because this comes from the soul, from the gut, or whatever you want to call it.

PRIDE LEADS YOU TO DISTRUST
EVERYTHING YOU DON'T UNDERSTAND.

Train your confidence: Send the email that's still sitting in the drafts folder; call the person you're too shy to contact; write that direct message; pen the poem; recite a verse in front of the mirror. These may seem like simple acts to you, but they're not trivial. Maybe you're more afraid of being told yes than of being told no. Do it and you will see how uncertainty reveals your hidden talents.

Make sure you don't deify joy, fame, or power, and refrain from mistreating, threatening, humiliating, or much less believing you're superior to, the failures of others simply because you are confident. We must balance both joys and sorrows equally and know that it is not about being perfect. Don't fake perfection; accept your vulnerability because it will also give you the confidence to be courageous.

Accept the light and the shadows to begin to live in confidence and integrity.

 ## SELF-AWARENESS

There's overwhelming evidence that individuals can make significant changes in their lives with willingness, confidence, and discipline. To foster these abilities, we must know ourselves well. That's why we must rely on tools to start internal exploration processes that help us understand how we behave and relate to others.

As we've seen, intrapersonal intelligence is a keen ability to interpret emotional activity: to anticipate, perceive, differentiate, and understand one's own feelings. This intelligence fuels a long list of actions, among which the following stand out:

- Efficiently managing feelings, emotions, and affections
- Finding resources for episodes of anxiety and distress
- Anticipating situations where support, solitude, or rest is needed

- Finding mechanisms to improve levels of willingness and confidence
- Adapting forms of communication to express what is felt
- Enjoying and making the most of each moment
- Recognizing when we are behaving inappropriately
- Being able to make self-critical evaluations
- Connecting with frustrations and wounds

If your intrapersonal intelligence is developed and you train it—like the naturally gifted musician who puts their heart and soul into studying their instrument—you will successfully take it to higher levels. But if it isn't developed, you must make an even greater effort to train it because you need to compensate for the limitations you have in that trait. This will help you make progress in your self-awareness. The best way to do this is by referring to behavioral models (discussed below).

When effectively understanding how the fabulous machinery of our being is programmed, we can take advantage of our intrapersonal intelligence, whether we have developed it or not. Knowing who we are facilitates the establishment of better communication mechanisms with others and allows us to reach a balance in which the ego surrenders in favor of a more fluid and honest relationship.

Behavioral science is complex, even when following all experimental rigors. Unlike the exact sciences, which allow us to control specific factors, human behavior is a tapestry woven from our fears, wounds, and experiences, even those that have lodged themselves in our unconscious. A scientific experiment, which can be done under controlled conditions or in a vacuum, is not the same as studying human beings, who cannot be isolated from the thousands of factors that influence them. Researchers create suitable conditions, but in no case will they be identical. You and I are—and will remain—a mystery.

I mention all of the above because human behavior cannot be predicted like the flight of migratory birds or the temperature at which certain liquids will boil. What we can know is a trend or a probability of occurrence. Before discussing behavioral models and self-awareness tools, it's crucial to keep the following in mind: Do not approach them superficially. Do not use them as absolute truths. And DO NOT (yes, in all caps) interpret them as a spreadsheet or a periodic table. These models are a guide that allows us to understand traits, strengths, and weaknesses, typical of some profiles, but they will never respond to absolute rules. And neither are they tarot cards or astrological rings that predict behavior. Do not make the mistake of pigeonholing or prejudging a person according to the results of a behavioral model.

EVERY DAY I THREATEN TO DYNAMITE REALITY WITH A SINGLE BLOW.

When someone knows their personality profile, they are better able to identify why they repeat certain behaviors. Psychology offers dozens of tools to determine these profiles, and through a point system they yield a preestablished result. Yet the key here is not which type, segment, or group we fall into, but how we use this information to continually improve ourselves through self-awareness.

When applying these tools, we need to carefully answer the questions in the assessments, taking the time to do so well and making sure we clearly understand the meaning of what is being asked. Since this is a numerical model, it doesn't think, it only provides answers based on the information you enter, which is why you must answer with the utmost honesty.

 ## ENNEAGRAMS

Among the many models available, I prefer those that combine simplicity (easy to apply and understand) with accessibility (abundant and reliable information). Some methodologies are theoretically robust but complex to apply, while others are very approachable but lack thorough results.

A good example of a tool that is simple to apply and widely accessible is the Enneagram. The term *enneagram* is a combination of two Greek words: *ennea*, which means "nine," and *gramma*, which refers to "something that's written or drawn"—in this case, a graphical model of nine lines. This tool aims to classify people into one of the nine predefined personality types (Enneagram types), emphasizing their relationship to one another. We can consider it a social tool because it mainly works using information based on relationship-associated behaviors.

This tool is so effective at describing human behavior that film academies use it to help writers develop powerful and consistent characters. In recent years, its popularity has grown so much that many readily available resources not only explore how it works but also its importance in subjects such as artistic creation, sexual behavior, emotional analysis, meditation, spiritual growth, and children's education.

Lately, its descriptive capacity for personal attitudes has caused such an impact that dozens of illustrated manuals have been published to understand children's behaviors, choose pets, and even as culinary guides based on each type. I also chose to share this tool with you because a growing number of specialists use it in their professional consultations.

My intention is that you mainly use it to discover and heighten your self-awareness.

ESSENCE WINS: IT IS INIMITABLE AND HAS NO COMPETITION.

The Enneagram is a Latin American contribution to the world. Although there were some initial attempts more than a hundred years ago, the modern structure, as it is used now, was developed through the independent yet collaborative research of Bolivian Oscar Ichazo and Chilean Claudio Naranjo. The latter, with more than thirty published works, had an outstanding impact in the United States.

Before we keep going, take a minute to remember this: There are no magic formulas. No method will give you the answers you're seeking—it will only help you find them. To avoid falling for this and other misconceptions, always keep the following in mind about the Enneagram types:

- *They are not absolute truths:* Knowing your type will not heal you. Use it as a guide to recognize and appreciate common traits, so that you can then learn how to compensate for the tendencies that might push you to make certain decisions.
- *We are not robots:* Even if someone matches a behavioral group, they never fit the described profile to a T and they

don't necessarily behave that way in every situation. What the Enneagram describes is behavioral tendencies and a coincidence in beliefs and values. We are human and we can make great changes, especially when we know ourselves better. We can always reinterpret and therefore redefine ourselves.

- *They do not define you; they only describe you:* Belonging to a specific group doesn't compel you to do anything, and it doesn't require you to change to fit the theory's description. Pretending to be different if you dislike your type isn't helpful either.
- *One Enneagram type isn't better than another:* No type is better or worse than another; they are just different, that's all. If at some point you find yourself favoring certain types over others, you may be unconsciously recalling figures in your life who fit those descriptions. This type of projection is natural but should be avoided.
- *This is not a game:* This is for you. Don't waste your time evaluating others because, in the end, even if you could do so successfully, you might not be able to do much with that. There's no point in evaluating someone if they aren't willing to change. By getting to know yourself better, you'll learn how to make better connections with others.
- *This is not a horoscope:* Avoid justifying other people's actions and decisions based on what you believe is their type. And avoid using this method to try to predict or justify your own actions. This is just a behavioral model. Your actions are based on your decisions, not your sign or your personality type. We'll explore decision-making further along in the book.

THE TRUTH HURTS

BUT LIES LEAVE SCARS.

- *Don't take anything for granted:* Reflect. After reviewing the assessment result, have a long conversation with yourself and use real events to explore how well you fit into your type. Remember, we're doing this to strengthen your intrapersonal intelligence and move forward in the inhalation process that will lead to your roar.

These recommendations are valid for all personality classification systems. The human being is a divine creation and enjoys the gift of diversity. There are only coincidences, tendencies, similarities. God does not create a series of figures with eight, twelve, or nine models. The only number we're interested in getting to know is one, which is within us. The objective of this study is unique and unrepeatable you.

IT TAKES GREAT STRENGTH TO
NOT FEAR OUR WEAKNESSES.

Now, let's get down to business. The graph below is the blueprint of relationships between the nine Enneagram types.

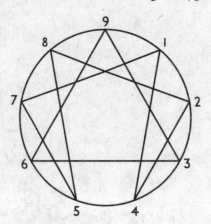

Each number on the graph represents an Enneagram type, which is associated with certain thinking, feeling, and behavioral traits. The lines that originate in each number show the relationship that type has with "neighboring" ones. According to this theory, people can emulate attitudes of the Enneagram types that are connected to their own. For instance, the graph shows that people belonging to Enneagram type 8 could adopt behaviors associated with types 5 or 2, which are connected to them, but we won't dive into this level of complexity here.

Many books name each Enneagram, but I prefer to refer to them by their number. By giving them a title, we attach an adjective to them, which can create bias. Since some names may be more appealing than others (achiever, individualist, helper), you may become impressionable. Words hold an intense power.

Our goal with this tool is to efficiently understand our strengths and weaknesses in different aspects of our life. Identifying where these patterns in our behavior come from will help us understand why we repeat some mistakes.

As you discover each type, you will likely associate it with someone you know. This is a very common reaction, but it must be carefully managed. For example, South African comedian Trevor Noah revealed in one of his shows that to imitate a country's accent, he copies the way one of his friends from that place speaks. In other words, he imitates one of his friends from Australia to represent all Australians, even if they don't all speak like that. His strategy is to take a sample and generalize it. He knows that not everyone sounds like his friend. When an Australian hears his imitation, they say, "I don't talk like that," but this imitation works for everyone else. You likely feel the same way when a person imitates someone from your country. This example shows you what can happen if you view all members of an Enneagram type through a reference point you think represents them. It may be useful as you get to know the model, because it'll help you remember each type's traits. However, not all Australians or French people talk like Noah's friends, and similarly, not all Enneagram type 6 individuals behave like the person you think belongs to that group. This gets even more complicated when the reference point you use belongs to someone you dislike, because negative biases may be intensified.

To determine our type, we must answer a series of questions. The most popular model has 15 questions for each type, totaling 135 questions. Make sure to set aside some time to do this. Quickly going through the questions is pointless. That will only waste your time, and you will waste even more time in your personal process of self-awareness. Do it with serenity, attention, and love.

WE NEVER EMERGE UNSCATHED
FROM CONVERSATIONS
WITH OURSELVES.

Be advised: I will explain each Enneagram type briefly because there are still many topics to cover in this book. I hope this information inspires you to delve deeper into the benefits of Enneagrams. This topic can be so vast that there are entire books dedicated to describing the traits of just one type.

When referring to people of different Enneagram types, I will abbreviate the name and use, for example, "E1" instead of "Enneagram Type 1."

ENNEAGRAM TYPE I ——————————————————

This profile tends to be rigid and has a strong sense of what they believe is right or wrong. They tend to be perfectionists in certain areas of their lives, which is very important to them. One could at times perceive a halo of superiority within this type.

They tend to be particularly severe with themselves and sharply critical of others. Oftentimes, this leads them to take control of situations, even when they don't involve them. They also tend to be more concerned with what can go wrong than with what may allow them to move forward.

They're hardworking and have issues with the middle ground. This may be one of the reasons why it's difficult for this type to let loose and enjoy themselves, although they're fun and eccentric when they do.

Two traits associated with this group are their tendency to experience anger episodes and their impatience. Their judgmental behavior usually isn't a good recipe for social relationships, especially when interacting with profiles that tend to feel attacked by other people's comments; despite the fact they are self-critical themselves. As you may have guessed, this excessive need for control can lead to a reluctance to be examined and an inability to accept other people's truths and imperfections.

ENNEAGRAM TYPE 2 ——————————————————

The second Enneagram type values strong social connections. They show a constant tendency to relate to others from that person's perspective. Their vibe usually finds a welcome space in the other and in satisfying the other even if they haven't been asked to do so.

When I was a kid, I had a classmate at school who always had extra pencils in his pencil case. Whenever one of us forgot a pencil and was about to face the teacher's scolding, he'd show up before being asked and offer one of his extra pencils, and he did it with great pleasure. Looking back, I realize I was in front of a full-fledged E2.

This constant devotion to giving is accompanied by an unconscious expectation of reward, which may not always be fulfilled. These behaviors may be accompanied by a belief that they give too much, and those who give too much usually expect the same in return.

These people give help without being asked for it. The need to help sometimes leads them to get involved in situations where they haven't been invited. They may put so much weight on everyone else's needs they find it hard to identify and, consequently, fulfill their own.

They're susceptible to being hurt because it's difficult for them to set limits with those who might take advantage of their need to help. This causes wounds that further deepen their need for approval.

THE WORST THING ABOUT A BIG HEART
IS THAT IT'S EASIER TO HIT.

ENNEAGRAM TYPE 3

I'd be pleased if there was an E3 reading this book right now, because their motivation is usually associated with actions that they feel will lead to success. Members of the other groups may read for entertainment or out of habit, but not E3s.

They display strong self-confidence and prioritize efficiency, which enables them to think and act with willpower to connect with what they want in the future. When they balance their strengths, they tend to be productive, persistent, and inspired.

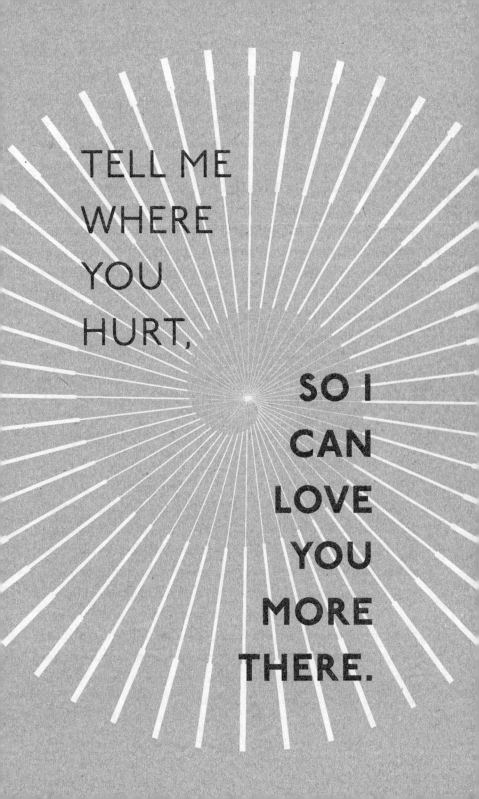

TELL ME WHERE YOU HURT, SO I CAN LOVE YOU MORE THERE.

They tend to be ambitious, proactive, and achievement-driven, but this also leads them to attach particular importance to status symbols. They find anything that has to do with possessions and positions stimulating. This can be accompanied by an aura of competitiveness that highlights those medals. The need for comparison gives special weight to things that are seen or demonstrated.

Since appreciation is measured by what they consider an achievement, and this is nothing more than a social construct, they end up giving priority to things that others find important. This valuation comes, of course, from the outside, from what they believe others think of them.

One of the great issues with this duality of execution (internal) and valuation (external) is that it can produce inner turmoil, because it can lead individuals to feel contempt for what they are if they don't have what they've worked so hard to get. The story of the naked emperor in the classic tale "The Emperor's New Clothes" is their worst nightmare.

ENNEAGRAM TYPE 4

This is a group that tends to be inward-focused, which is why they may be considered individualistic. They compensate for this introspection with a certain amount of overreaction. So, they can appear dramatic or romantic, and their hypersensitivity isn't just emotional, it can also manifest itself in their physical and mental health.

These are people who perceive themselves as different from those around them. This difference, or self-exclusion, makes them view themselves as outsiders in their environment, and they enjoy this and reinforce it with their behavior—as a rule, they even reflect it in their physical appearance and general tastes.

They exhibit a penchant for creativity. This doesn't mean that all members of this group are artistic and that the other Enneagram types are lacking artists. It simply means that they tend to be sensitive and creative.

The introspective, exaggerated, and creative combo is a double-edged sword when it comes to interpersonal relationships. They tend to construct stories and hyperbolize certain feelings, which makes them more susceptible to disillusionment, increasing their abandonment wounds and their need to seek refuge in individualism. When analyzing them, we must consider that people who feel misunderstood may also have difficulties understanding others.

By insisting that no one understands them, they may be the most reluctant to accept their type. E4s reading this paragraph may question how a personality model can summarize what they have failed to resolve throughout their lives. *Capisce?*

WE DO NOT NEED SPRING
FOR US TO BLOOM.

ENNEAGRAM TYPE 5

If you were one of those children who, instead of playing with friends in the neighborhood, preferred to be at home, looking things up in books or experimenting with insects in your garden, you will understand the most remarkable attribute of this group.

They are known for having an innovative vision and enjoying complex activities. They prefer knowledge over action; in other words, they like learning details about the sea more than taking a dip in it.

This knowledge, this passion for the abstract, keeps them a

little distant from the concrete, but they don't go unnoticed. They have the impulse to demonstrate how much they know, much like how E3s brag about their accomplishments or possessions. This is a form of validation that comes from outside approval, which largely conditions how they interact socially. For E5s, knowing isn't as important as having others validate how much they know.

Their knowledge—which, as we've seen, is different from intelligence—doesn't necessarily translate into emotional skills. It can actually serve as a shield that stops them from making a deep connection with their most sensitive side. This affects their ability to understand feelings, pain, and fears, because no matter how prepared they are, theories won't be help them comprehend these emotions.

They tend to be reserved and to limit their relationships to close-knit circles, where they shine. On the outside, they express an aversion to affection, even though they depend on human contact as much as everyone else. Let's never forget that knowing a lot doesn't mean knowing what is best for us.

ENNEAGRAM TYPE 6

This is a complex description. Those who fit in this group are defensive and cautious, but worthy of the trust given to them.

They tend to seek external support for decision-making. This is a sign of a potential need to find self-confidence. They depend on external approval when they must take steps that are indispensable for their growth. In other words, although they insist that they know themselves, they often doubt how they'll get out of what they can't control. This means that they're particularly susceptible to catastrophic thinking, which makes them organized planners, but not necessarily executors. Living in a state of perpetual caution invites them to constantly procrastinate. They often try to be prepared at all times, but this doesn't necessarily lead them to complete the tasks they commit to. Their wounds are mainly associated with injustice issues, and they tend to assume heroic positions in those available spaces.

What mobilizes a person who is always anticipating a potential shipwreck? Well, dry land, because even a calm sea is a risk to be avoided. Losing their comfort is something they don't even want to talk about. They seek confirmation of their ideas among those around them, so they willingly accept authority and guidelines. Having the support and guidance of others is like having an anchor on solid ground, so there's a marked fear of finding themselves in situations without the support of their guides.

I BELIEVE IN LOYALTY
**WHEN NO ONE
IS WATCHING YOU.**

ENNEAGRAM TYPE 7

This group consists of energetic people who aren't afraid to experiment and take risks. This explosive tendency has an inconsistent and scattered side.

They can be described as "the life of the party." They have an enthusiastic attitude that leads them to enjoy adventures, but not necessarily get hooked on them. Their festive disposition and raucous happiness may help to avoid certain wounds. On the other hand, their focus on the immediate takes them away from an inner connection that requires peace and calm.

They insist that other people join their "crusade" of pleasures, even if that means having to give up formalities and labels. They regularly clash with pessimistic and even realistic positions.

Constantly seeking pleasure doesn't translate to inner satisfaction, although it could come off that way. This playful aspect doesn't mean that they live on the road or at parties—it represents how they channel the way they perform their tasks and commitments. E7s may lose interest and become disengaged when relationships, work, or study no longer provide the same initial satisfaction and entertainment. This is a problem because everything, even the things we like the most, go through less exciting phases.

This group avoids activities that limit their freedom, such as situations they find routine, monotonous, or arduous, even if they're necessary conditions to achieve their goals. Therefore, it's likely that the members of this group are busy people, yet not always constant.

ENNEAGRAM TYPE 8

They are described as people with a high tendency to exercise self-reliance and control. In fact, they often have the natural ability to establish the independence they desire because they enjoy inherent resources.

That "strength" doesn't make them invincible—although they try to project a dominant image, they're actually as docile as everyone else—but this insistence closes the floodgates of their emotional dam. It's not easy for them to show openness because doing so may reveal part of that fragility they prefer to keep hidden behind a protective armor, which makes them feel unflappable even though they aren't.

They invest most of their energy in winning and imposing their

YOU
THOUGHT
YOU WERE
LOST

AND YOU
FOUND
YOURSELF IN
GOD.

vision, which pushes them to engage in discussions and debates on even the most basic issues. They don't easily give in, especially regarding intellectual matters.

Just as they're willing to argue over the smallest detail, their sense of power leads them to want to protect those they feel are under their authority, because it's a way of demonstrating it.

They're protective but also especially wary of the possibility of betrayal. This is the worst thing that can happen to those who feel the intense need to exercise power and be righteous because it implies a discrediting of their authority, in which they find validation.

Many important historic figures embody this Enneagram type. There are notable examples of great leaders who have brought about significant changes in their nations, including several figures who have led their peoples down good paths and, unfortunately, several who have led their peoples down evil paths.

SOME PEOPLE GET UPSET WITH YOU
BECAUSE YOU LOVE YOURSELF.

ENNEAGRAM TYPE 9 ───────────

There's a reason this group is the last one on the list. E9s position themselves here because it's where they're least exposed and have the lowest chance of conflict. They struggle to resolve conflict and avoid at all costs bearing the brunt of a confrontation.

They're known for wanting peace of mind and are not willing to trade it for a potentially tense situation. To avoid conflict they will tend to say yes, even if they'd prefer to say no.

"If I remove myself from the equation, there is no conflict" would be one of the formulas with which this group tries to resolve their issues. And it may sound logical, but it isn't. They just end up avoiding conflict with others, not with themselves. Every "unfought war" turns into an accumulated defeat. This drags on and becomes increasingly burdensome.

They can be identified as calm, cordial, discreet people. This isn't just superficial; they behave more or less the same on the inside because they find it difficult to reflect. The fact that they can be a little self-conscious in how they express themselves and frequently relinquish control doesn't mean they create emotional distance. Many of the people in this Enneagram type are empathetic and can tune in emotionally with a certain ease. In fact, the norm is that they can skillfully interpret other people's emotions but struggle to decipher their own. In any case, living in a constant state of concession can also create distortions in communication; one-sided relationships can't be fruitful.

After this short introduction to the Enneagram types, you have an important task: to take an Enneagram assessment and identify your predominant personality type. To do so, go online and find a reputable Enneagram test. Take your time to complete the assessment—it will play an important role in your future performance. Answer as honestly as possible and don't try to respond with the intention of fitting a particular Enneagram type. Remember what we mentioned about mathematical instruments: They're developed only to fulfill the model's specifications. If you answer what you wish to be true rather than the truth, this test will be useless because you won't be able to rely on its revelations.

Once you have the result, take a moment to examine it and quietly reflect whether it fits you. Focus specifically on the positive aspects and motivations. A person's identity is made up of "good" and "bad" traits, balancing deficiencies and excesses.

Do this exercise for yourself—don't waste energy putting labels on the people in your life until you finish internalizing what this means for your process. Don't assume someone's type based on a few observed behaviors. Remember what I said before: We are not robots. Hasty assessments are nothing more than seeing through the lenses of your prejudices. If you take this tool seriously, you'll notice that one of its greatest benefits is understanding the relationships between the different types.

So how does knowing your Enneagram type affect the possibility of accumulating the power of a roar? The answer lies in the fact that self-awareness is essential to understanding the origins of the limitations that haven't allowed you to emerge or have limited your progress. This will in turn help you to get to know the origin of those patterns that you repeat time and again without understanding why.

AN OSCAR
FOR MY INTUITION.

Take these inner journeys and look at yourself in these mirrors, if possible, with professional assistance, which will help you quickly identify the areas you need to challenge. Doing systematic self-evaluations and looking at ourselves with discipline is a step toward understanding how we think, feel, and act. That is the starting point for our realignment; it fills our chest with the possibility of exploding.

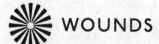 ## WOUNDS

Accepting reality is one of the most demanding tasks a human being can face, but if you don't do it, you will lose your way and miss out on moving toward your goals. We often choose to stay where we suffer the most. Although moving from there is a logical alternative, we don't know why we resist it and remain immobile. This puts us in situations that harm us while we don't even attempt to defend ourselves.

After reviewing the Enneagram results, you may wonder why you fall into one type and not another; you may feel that your life history and the type of education you've received should put you in a different Enneagram type than the one that best describes your behavior. That inconsistency is confusing, but we'll discuss this later. Remember: When you compare yourself, you distort yourself.

We can find the explanation in the wounds we've accumulated and often don't know we have. Discovering and identifying the wound is a fundamental part of its healing. We've discussed identifying our personality style, but sometimes those tendencies to demonstrate what we have or what we know, that need to exercise authority or to be competent, are ways of trying to hide the scars that our wounds have left behind. Those scars often influence who we are because our personality is attempting to reassert itself or run away from them.

We accumulate scars from birth (several authors say that this begins to happen even before we are born). The cracks that gradually fracture the soul are formed in the first six years of life. For more than four decades, the author Lise Bourbeau has referred to five main wounds: rejection, abandonment, humiliation, betrayal, and injustice.[2] According to Bourbeau, they shape our internal dialogue regarding the judgments we make, especially our self-judgment. This theory is widely accepted and applied throughout the world.

If a person's life is affected by one of their wounds, some of their fears, concerns, and emotions will be strongly associated with it. For example, rejection, which often happens in the first months of life, will shape some of our concepts of self-esteem, satisfaction, and interpretation of interpersonal relationships. The rejection wound will not be the only component defining these concepts; there will be other factors and experiences that will help shape your image, but its contribution will be resounding if you don't take action to heal it.

You can minimize the scars left by a wound by developing good habits and frequent self-reflection. But if you give that wound power, and it weighs heavily on your perception of reality, you'll start to question your own worth, which will lead to low self-esteem, shame, and unfulfilling comparisons with others.

WOUNDS HAVE EYES,
BUT DON'T USE THEM TO SEE.
USE THE ONES YOU HAVE IN YOUR SOUL.

Following is an example of how this works using a recent case, one of those moments when life seems to be writing a comedy. Someone I know asked for my advice, which has become part of my job, and I accept it with great pleasure. When we spoke, he suddenly blurted out that he was having an affair. The situation was tormenting him because, although he wanted to start a stable relationship with this other person, he didn't dare leave his wife, considering all the suffering this would cause her and the rest of his family.

To justify his actions, he clung mainly to the fear of what others might say, how his children would take it, and causing his wife too much suffering.

I then asked him several questions, which he had to answer for himself, to reveal certain core truths. I turned what he thought would be a cleansing session that would relieve him of guilt into an opportunity to explore his reasoning. What began as a quick chat over coffee became several hours of deep talk, and after many increasingly profound questions, we found a little light in all the darkness and discovered the real reason that prevented him from acting: He was afraid that his wife and children would continue to be happy without him or, worse, with someone else. He was trapped in an absurd need for approval. He couldn't stand the possibility of being compared with someone else and losing. His rejection wound pushed him to run away from the problem and remain tied to a reality that made him unhappy.

The conquistador who benevolently gave up his happiness so that others wouldn't feel pain was instead trapped in the fear that his departure would be beneficial for the one he said he "didn't love anymore." Trapped in a web spun by his own ego, he was unhappy with his relationship, but he dared not leave because if his wife didn't suffer, his self-concept would suffer. If she rebuilt her life, that would mean he was expendable. In short, he couldn't face the truth about himself.

I know I mentioned this earlier, but I want to repeat it: Accepting a reality like this one is an extremely difficult task. Once again, the truth hurts, but it's liberating. To deny that inhaling helps heal our wounds is like believing we can cure ourselves of cancer without allowing the doctors to examine the tumor. That is why it's so important to start by getting to know ourselves.

 ## MASKS

Wounds can condition certain behaviors and shape them in such a way that they become an integral part of us. It's worth clarifying that they aren't necessarily produced by concrete events, but by how we interpret them.

I know you may not think you have "suffered" a particular injury. Yet there are some, such as the abandonment wound, that are said to take shape in the first years of life. Perhaps in your early childhood you had no reason to feel abandonment; you had loving parents who were there for you, so you're reluctant to accept that you've sustained that wound. However, the issue isn't just about what your parents did but how you interpreted their actions. Some people were physically or emotionally abandoned, while others accumulated wounds because their parents were far away due to work responsibilities or even because of death. These circumstances seep in through the filter that shapes our wounds and defines our personality. At the same time, not everyone who suffers abandonment, even in the strictest sense of the word, endures serious emotional injuries.

People may say things like "I couldn't have been hurt by my mother, because I didn't have one," as if such an absence is not a violent enough act to hurt you. The pain can be there even if that absence was involuntary, even if the absent person was loving during the time they shared with you.

On one hand, there's the issue of who we choose to put in the role of the absent person. Many people who grew up without a father emphasize "not having" a father figure. But at an age when our wounds are still developing, we subconsciously choose others to take that place, and their influence leaves a definite mark on us: grandfathers, uncles, or other children's fathers.

As can be seen from the previous abandonment wound example, the construction and assimilation of wounds can be very different even though they seem to have the same origin. Two people with the same stimuli can respond in totally different ways. A loving and consistent parent can come from either a harmonious or a broken home. We don't know how the wounds that intoxicate our ego were created, yet this is the orchestra conductor of our main actions.

SOMETIMES DARKNESS REVEALS TRUTHS THAT CANNOT BE SEEN IN THE LIGHT.

We all believe that our anxieties are unique to us, when in fact co-incidences abound. That's why Bourbeau sums up each person's responses to their wounds by saying that they lead to behavioral patterns which allow us to identify them. The theory suggests that each wound has a primary response called a "mask," which is a compensatory mechanism people use to cope with the damage.

Let's go back to the case of the man who was being unfaithful and who discovered that his deepest fear was not being needed by his family. As a result of our conversation, I was able to confirm that he suffered from the rejection wound, which came from believing he didn't fulfill the necessary requirements to be loved. Carrying that wound can create a reactive force to negative evaluations and criticism. The search for approval and recognition can lead such individuals to repeatedly trip over the same stone or to think that the stones are the ones that trip *them* up. They want support, but don't know how to handle the excessive attention, so they end up taking on an evasive attitude, which is why their mask, their primary response, is "flight."

But the issues arising from this wound are not limited to the relationship scenario. This willingness to dismiss criticism, seek approval everywhere, and avoid any situation where you may be evaluated, will carry over into other areas of your life. These behaviors can prevent you from taking on new positions, cultivating friendships, or changing roles.

Can you imagine how jealous someone must feel when their wounds prevent them from seeking happiness in a new situation because they can't bear the thought of someone else being happy in their absence? How much fear of dying can there be in these cases?

Like the man tempted by an affair, we each have our own wounds. For some, they're so visible it's impossible to miss them. For others, finding them requires work. Therefore, as bestselling author Lise Bourbeau suggested, you'll find a corresponding mask for each type of wound, so that you can easily identify if you suffer from any of them.[3]

For example, withdrawal is a mask for rejection. Dependence is a mask for abandonment. Control is a mask for betrayal. Rigidity is a mask for injustice. Masochism is a mask for humiliation.

The ego can feed you lies to keep you from experiencing pain. It's so fragile there is no choice but to treat it like a child. It's simply afraid of being humiliated, mistreated, or abandoned, but it's clumsy and tends to knock over whatever crosses its path.

YOUR SOUL
SAYS
YOUR
EGO
IS THE ONE
WHO IS
AFRAID.

Let's return to the importance of self-awareness to explore whether we comply with pre-established patterns that allow us to identify our deepest ailments. Several of these answers are much clearer when we use self-assessment tools, such as the Enneagram we've already discussed. Now, instead of analyzing the descriptions of each type, let's look at the main currents within them that can lead us into turbulent seas.

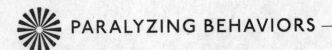 ## PARALYZING BEHAVIORS

I hope that by now you've done the test I suggested on page 47 and that you already know your Enneagram type.

I'm assuming you followed my recommendation and carefully analyzed each question and answered with complete honesty. Then you read the results and compared them with your inner motivations. I hope the descriptions respond to your desires, your fears, and the way you relate to others. If you haven't taken an Enneagram test yet, stop reading and take the time to do it before moving on.

I HAVE PLENTY OF LIGHT BECAUSE
I DON'T SEEK TO OUTSHINE ANYONE.

This new perspective, along with what we now know about wounds and the masks we wear to hide them, is the arsenal we'll use to face the inner battle of getting to know ourselves, until we can see ourselves clearly. For example, each Enneagram type may display certain behaviors that can stop them from achieving their dreams.

BEHAVIORS THAT PARALYZE
ENNEAGRAM TYPE 1 ————————————————

As perfectionists, E1s tend to be critical and eager to fix what others have done. Eternally dissatisfied, perfection is another way of running away from themselves. Emotionally, they tend to focus on their sense of duty over what their heart demands, with all the consequences that come with going down that path. Their fixation on criticism leads to "self-judgment" where their ego keeps saying: "If I were you, I would have done it this way . . ." This makes them feel misunderstood. Change becomes complex for them because they end up throwing away their accumulated effort. The ego realizes that admitting mistakes or changing course is a loss: "If you do it, everyone will see your seams." As always, the task is to convince it otherwise. Their greatest fear is that their threads and seams will show.

BEHAVIORS THAT PARALYZE
ENNEAGRAM TYPE 2 ————————————————

Although E2s don't think about it consciously, they expect reciprocity for what they do. They leave an outstanding debt. They must convince themselves that retribution is not the only way to find value. They find it difficult to do things for themselves, without it resulting in inner conflict, and thus make transcendental decisions based on not disappointing other people, like a mother who decides not to study at night so she can take care of her family instead. They wait for recognition in vain because they insist on valuing what they give with a bill of exchange that no one knows about and that often doesn't come through. They are enslaved by a void.

BEHAVIORS THAT PARALYZE
ENNEAGRAM TYPE 3 ——————————————

When individuals insist on perceiving their self-worth based on their possessions or accomplishments instead of their desires or emotions, they become blocked, especially when it comes to decisions related to more intimate matters. There is a latent tendency to avoid being seen as they are; this activates the possibility of projecting distorted images and losing authenticity. They'll find it hard to abandon the spaces where they stand out, which could paralyze them in mediocre environments. They may close themselves off to alternatives, like exploring options where they feel that comparisons may be unfavorable. The ego repeats, "You are what you achieve," but they must be convinced that there is much more value in being.

BEHAVIORS THAT PARALYZE
ENNEAGRAM TYPE 4 ——————————————

E4s are defined by hypersensitivity and end up forming scabs. They may be reluctant to interact with people who could make their worst perspectives come true. They could live in a state of continuous reflection, always looking inward and constantly criticizing themselves. They find it difficult to expose themselves and open up completely, as they might be misunderstood. Overreaction increases that feeling. Understandably, this increases their dependence on the people they trust, and that can become distressful. Their biggest challenge will likely be to convince their ego to enjoy what they have, even when the experiences do not turn out as expected. The shadow of abandonment can keep them tied to situations that cause them enormous pain.

BEHAVIORS THAT PARALYZE
ENNEAGRAM TYPE 5 ———————————————————

These individuals will shy away from large groups, especially if their thoughts remain silent, if they become irrelevant, or if no one listens to them. They'll think twice before taking any steps that may put them in situations where they have to express their feelings because their ego considers emotional dependence risky. This will affect their decision-making because their thought patterns will come up with a thousand excuses to avoid situations where they're out of their depth, like places where they may encounter people who know more than they do. They justify their actions by saying that they don't want to be exposed, but they're really avoiding being compared to others. New environments or situations where they feel comfortable are ideal for them.

BEHAVIORS THAT PARALYZE
ENNEAGRAM TYPE 6 ———————————————————

This group is particularly susceptible to catastrophic thinking. Even when things are on the right track, they may find a reason to back out of their intentions. Their distrust leads them to sail on calm seas, far from emotional tempests. Many of their decisions are called off for this reason. They frequently impair their judgment by seeking the approval of those around them. Betrayals, rejections, conflicts, or abandonment are the gales they most want to avoid, but they especially dread being alone. Many mistakes are made for this reason.

BEHAVIORS THAT PARALYZE
ENNEAGRAM TYPE 7 ────────────────

This group struggles to participate in situations they cannot easily get out of, where they lose their options. They're so focused on what they stand to lose that they don't spend time evaluating the opportunities to win. They will give up if they feel they may lose their freedom or fall into a routine, monotonous, or demanding process, yet all of these conditions are necessary to accomplish a good part of their objectives. They may always be busy, which doesn't mean they're constant people, and so much noise around them prevents them from being able to listen to themselves and accept that goals, especially at the beginning, require a certain dose of discomfort.

BEHAVIORS THAT PARALYZE
ENNEAGRAM TYPE 8 ────────────────

These individuals struggle to make decisions that require openness because it reveals part of a fragility they prefer to conceal behind an armor, which makes them feel powerful, even if they aren't. Their ego has convinced them that setting their emotions aside helps them demonstrate authority. They feel uncomfortable in situations where they may lose power. They put pressure on themselves to protect others over their own needs for friendship, support, or companionship. They must convince themselves that deciding not to be in charge is also a demonstration of strength.

BEHAVIORS THAT PARALYZE
ENNEAGRAM TYPE 9 ————————————————

One of the great challenges for this group is to understand that in order to achieve what they want, they must endure bumps in the road. It's impossible to make decisions without expecting them. Yet E9s believe that their thoughts, actions, or contributions don't matter; therefore, when they want to take action or move forward, they fear they might be rejected or humiliated, so they stay put. The message within them should point to individual commitment, to an analysis of their previous results, when choosing submission didn't generate profits.

By redefining your talents and identifying the tendencies that may be holding you back, you begin an internal search that may change the course of your destiny, if you so desire. Along the way, you'll be able to choose from thousands of psychological, academic, and mystical concepts that will justify why things haven't turned out as you'd like, but none of them carry more weight than what you're capable of finding in yourself. It doesn't matter if you've made mistakes related to psychological types or esoteric ideas of predestination—you must put your own insights first, because there is no reality more forceful than the one that comes from your own thoughts and actions.

SIGHT IS TO **RECOGNIZE WHAT YOU LOVE**
BEFORE YOU CAN SEE IT.

My life has several purposes, and one of them is to help you break down the obstacles that prevent you from moving forward on a new path.

☀ CONSISTENCY AND AUTHENTICITY ───────

Our conscious and unconscious wounds produce words that we use to develop our thoughts and understand reality. As we accumulate wounds, we begin to build a vocabulary that eventually becomes a rigid language loaded with biases. The way we speak to ourselves and about ourselves does not just condition our ideas and paths, it also creates emotions that impact our behavioral patterns, our mood, and even our DNA. On the flip side, recognizing this language can help us identify our unconscious wounds by revealing the incompatibility between the vocabulary we've built over the years and our deepest desires.

Some of the conflicts we carry with us are related to the disconnect between internal concepts and recurring behaviors. We need to be consistent, and not being so makes us extremely uncomfortable. Knowing our type can help us reconcile our self-image with the attitudes that lead us to contradict it.

Several psychological theories suggest that human beings need to be consistent in life; in other words, our thoughts and actions naturally seek coherence and, to a certain extent, our sense of stability depends on it. This can lead us to completely rewrite the information we receive, the motivation for our behavior, and even how we remember our own past.

I WRITE ABOUT BLOWS
I CANNOT GIVE..

I know it sounds great to say you're consistent; it's something you can proudly include on your résumé. But sometimes great changes

I'M SEARCHING FOR

ALL THE
PROMISES
WE MADE TO
OURSELVES.

come from questioning what we never question. That's why it's good to ask ourselves if it's worth preserving a trait that takes us away from who we want to be. I know dozens of people who have chosen to dress up as intellectuals and therefore believe that pursuing activities they consider "superficial" would be "inconsistent" with who they are, even though these activities could end the lonely lives they don't always admit they want to change. That desire for consistency is the first obstacle they need to face. This is a fairly simple example; I'm sure you know several similar ones.

I'm not trying to say that a person should behave erratically, or that they shouldn't be consistent between what they offer and what they deliver. What I mean is that the quest to remain consistent with the image we've created of ourselves, at any cost, can become a mask that obscures our view of who we really want to be.

Knowing ourselves and seeing ourselves without our ego's arbitration allows us to reconcile who we are with the distorted image of who we think we are. We suffer so intensely because we believe things should be the way our ego assumes they should be. We're so attached to our views that if we could just step back with some degree of objectivity, many of our egocentric ideas would make us cringe and embarrass us.

This view of consistency doesn't mean you should give up honesty, integrity, or spontaneity, because this issue has to do with behaviors and beliefs that define the image you have imposed on yourself. You may say that you do it for yourself, that it comes from you, but that thought can be challenged by the fact that often we can only feel "consistent" if others perceive us that way. If you were to travel somewhere tomorrow where no one knows you, and you behaved differently than usual, no one would notice, and as a result you might not feel any conflict within you.

Consistency involves not only your actions but also your thoughts, so a change in your core beliefs creates a significant rupture. The idea is to prevent you from falling into the pit known as "dissonance," a concept you may be familiar with from my previous books or videos. Dissonance occurs when our behaviors do not align with our beliefs or our discourse.

In that case, the first truth you must challenge is whether you seek consistency for you or for what others ask of you, for how they perceive you. We greatly value this attribute because we have trained our environment with a script featuring a character we play, not ourselves. The character has devoured the person.

Suppose you are in an everyday setting, but no one knows you. For example, you're at work, but your colleagues have no idea who you are yet. Now reflect on this: Would you change anything in the way you act? Would you free yourself from any particular situation?

Think about the differences between your behavior in those circumstances and now. If there are changes you want to make, why haven't you made them? Are you trying to maintain consistency? Are you afraid that how others perceive you will change?

Don't confuse consistency with authenticity. Both are intrinsic needs of the human being, close but not identical. The first tends to lead us to our beliefs and attitudes; the second, to our identity. Different but essential to our relationships with others because people need to have a general idea of how we think, but they also need to know that they're interacting with someone who is who they say they are.

LIFE WILL ALWAYS GIVE YOU NEW OPPORTUNITIES
(TO MAKE MISTAKES AGAIN).

Just as the Enneagram types describe the way we relate to others, consistency and authenticity are realities that are framed by our interactions with others. When we succeed in changing our behavior to align with our desires, it's important to establish a renewed consistency by breaking the one we have and replacing it with a new one. Yet the most significant step is when our change is in line with God's plan for us.

 ## SHAME AND GUILT

There are two concepts that we often confuse in everyday speech: shame and guilt. Both are emotions. Shame has an internal relationship with our being, with who we are rather than what we do. It often comes up when we compare our actions or circumstances to those of others, but it really stems from our own vision. Guilt is more commonly associated with the outcome of our actions. It's the difference between who we are and what we do.

Shame becomes a viper within us, injecting its venom and turning us into beings who hide from others. This concealment not only happens through shyness, withdrawal, or constant embarrassment, but also through lies and a distorted version of who we are, so that we can hide where no one would think to look for

I PREFER TO REPAIR THAN TO REPLACE.

us: right where we are. This disguise may work on others, but it shouldn't fool the person staring back at us in the mirror, whom we're also trying to deceive.

Overwhelming shame sweeps away the joy of being who we are, ruins our relationship with ourselves, and erases any traces of the roads we've paved for ourselves, sinking them into the sludge of self-pity, apathy, and compulsive cowardice. We cannot bet on ourselves if we believe we are losers.

We must limit the weight of this emotion and how it affects us because social pressure alone can force us to feel shame for who we are, not because we've done something wrong or our behavior is inappropriate, but because we clash with the established norms. We cannot, for example, let others condemn us for our past just because our present is better than theirs. There are many wounds that can be caused by a situation that makes us feel out of place, like second-class passersby in life. And that reality continues to play out with respect to issues of financial and educational standing. And once started, the morality sentinels will continue dabbing their sponges in vinegar to irritate the lesions of the newly condemned.

THOSE WHO THINK OF THEMSELVES
AS SAINTS STOPPED FOLLOWING ME
BECAUSE I WAS A HERETIC.
**SO WHY ARE THESE "CLEAN ONES"
READING SOMEONE AS DIRTY AS ME?**

Constantly thinking about the filter through which others perceive you permanently subjects you to guilt, and not allowing yourself to enjoy being who you are robs you of the opportunity to savor your life. Living with the obsession of trying to fit in for approval will sink your audacity into the swamp of standards you did not meet. Shame leads you to think beforehand that authenticity will limit how much others like you. You want to feel that you belong to the groups you've put in charge. Leaving their orbits, even if they were always unnatural to you, goes against the identity you have created. And those groups only want you as long as you are being what they want you to be.

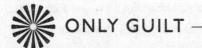 ## ONLY GUILT

Guilt often knocks the wind out of us before the roar. It's usually accompanied by a need for repair, even if it's not done in the right way. I wonder if this is one of its positive sides. Who hasn't thought about it? Everyone seeks to atone for their guilt, whether in religion, philosophy, law, history, anthropology, psychology, or poetry. It's the child of all those reflections, born of love and hate.

Guilt gave rise to rites, meditations, prayers, dogmas, cries, sacrifices, and penances. Is there forgiveness without guilt? Throughout the world we hear incessant murmurs saying, "It's my fault," "It's his fault," "It wasn't my fault." Does that bring us comfort?

We naturally feel guilt when we do something we believe is wrong, when we hurt someone, when we go against our values, when we give in to what we promised to avoid. We feel guilt for lies, betrayal, negligence, and irreverence. And it makes sense to feel this way about all that. But there are also those who feel guilty about situations beyond their control, such as their parents' divorce or a mishap with a friend, or even when good things happen to them, such as being happy or doing well on the test others failed. We carry painful guilt, such as not being able to do anything for a loved one who took their own life.

CHRIST CLEANSED US FROM OUR GUILT, AND
WE CLEANSE OUR GUILT FROM CHRIST.

Guilt doesn't hurt, but it does do harm; it doesn't produce fear, but it makes us flee; it may be about something that happened in the past, but it is still present. Sometimes I believe we carry Adam and Eve's guilt in our genes, a shame that has seeped into society as a whole. It's like an organ that humans cannot remove, a compass that gives us direction, a mark that only erases the genuine reception of Christ. Was it not He who transformed the weight of our guilt, paying in advance for all repentance?

Can I find myself in what makes me feel guilty? Does it watch over what prevents me from entering my unconscious, protecting me from the truth that I do not wish to accept? It has erected a wall right in the middle our fragile freedom. How do we deal, for example, with the guilt that society puts on us for being born with gifts, talents, or privileges?

Guilt can be a path of self-learning, but we must overcome it, because if we let it grow, it will produce a cancer in the bowels of our internal perception. As mentioned earlier, guilt can lead us to a constant state of trying to compensate, to pay capital on an insatiable debt, and this is not always a luxury we can afford, especially because being consumed by guilt makes it harder to feel empathy for others who have done wrong. I believe that a certain percentage of this emotion can play a role in making us more aware of our mistakes or help us intervene in them, and thus repair or adjust our steps. It is like a recalibrating tool.

Guilt never travels alone; it always moves in a group. Its friends are anguish, frustration, sadness, and the least productive thoughts of the human being. It becomes a broken record in different dimensions of time. It perverts our moral judgment, it's accompanied by experts with subjective and biased opinions, it confuses our behavior, it makes us believe that self-imposed punishment will save us. Remorse isn't the same as repentance. The former is a desire, the latter, a fact. The former is a temporary behavioral change, while the latter produces a change in your nature. Keep an eye on guilt and don't allow it to corrupt your reality, making you fall into an agonizing tempest.

What good is a guilt that we have no use for? In most cases it only torments us without contributing anything. We have been taught to feel it, and that includes a long list of social, familial, cultural, and primarily religious norms that pertain more to others than to ourselves. We've also been made to feel guilty about what others don't want us to feel. They want us to feel bad for knowing without having a diploma, for believing without receiving the handler's lashes, for loving without following their moral, dogmatic, and religious norms.

RELIGIOSITY IS ONE OF **GUILT'S** **FAVORITE HOTELS**.

I must admit that I've been hurt by my desire to comply with the narcissistic idea of perfection imposed by religiosity, which forgets I belong to the kingdom of God not by deeds but by grace. I believe that people who consider themselves saints tend to sweep their faults under the rug of their hypocrisy, even if sooner or later they're discovered. Pretending to be perfect suffocates you; the mirror doesn't lie and it reflects an image that slaps you in the face.

One of the best strategies I have found to move forward in the face of guilt is to master the limits of my responsibility. This foundation has helped me identify all the thoughts and behaviors that make me feel guilty—it's the only way I've been able to detect their nuances and effects. Another fundamental point is to learn that my mistakes are not a prison sentence, nor a sign of incompetence or loss. Expressing my emotions with my loved ones has always been a good source of comfort in the face of my mistakes.

 ## WHERE TO FIND SUPPORT ────

"It was my fault." Belting out those words seems simple, but the abyss between regret and remorse is an entire universe. Acknowledging one's mistake and assuming the resulting responsibilities is one of the most dismal territories an individual can cross. To acknowledge this, we must change our attitude. That change is the leap we must take into the void, but guilt prevents us from realizing it.

We can't deny it: We have an inexhaustible creativity for finding excuses and ignoring mistakes. We have a PhD in escaping consequences, but guilt has a fascinating trick: It doesn't chase you, it attracts you.

Playing the role of the innocent victim, believing that we always pay for other people's mistakes, is the strategy we adopt as a defense mechanism to avoid taking our own absolute and nontransferable responsibility. After a self-critical process, sincere acknowledgment is a sign not only of maturity and wisdom but also of a vast soul and profound heart.

Acknowledging our mistake and acting accordingly prepares us to make amends. It will not always be enough for others; that makes sense, but only by removing the eternal punishment of guilt will we move forward in the attempt to repair the damage, including the one we do to ourselves.

We can alleviate the mistake and guilt by lovingly releasing our feelings with trust. Sin grows stronger when we keep it to ourselves; confession weakens it, but this merits a safe place, because confessions make you vulnerable—by opening the doors of your soul, you expose yourself to endless wounds.

This reflection leads me to ask myself: Do my family, my friends, my colleagues, my partner provide a safe space where I can be vulnerable? In many cases, the answer is a painful no. We live in a state of excessive judgment that muzzles those who need grace. It's the terror of being imprisoned, lynched for your sins. It's the absurd demand of perfection, judged by a bunch of other imperfect people who think they hold the bar for measuring holiness. When the heart is cold, it can only be warmed by love and mercy.

HE TURNED THE OTHER CHEEK, AND I GAVE HIM A KISS.

Jesus said "go!" but we have become used to demanding that others "come." If we haven't experienced mercy in our lives, for our sins and angsts, how can we be merciful? That's why we've become used to attacking others, their indiscretions and offenses, and especially the sins they've committed, which we haven't taken responsibility for in our own lives. Their sin may remind us of our own and create tension within us—a tension that seeks to soften our shame and exacerbate our guilt.

We must learn to enjoy our ability to show mercy. "Confess therefore your sins one to another, and pray one for another, that ye may be healed. The supplication of a righteous man availeth much in its working," according to the wisdom of James 5:16. To embody a perfection that doesn't exist does God a disservice: It confuses His message and hurts humanity.

If you feel that guilt is overtaking you, if you believe that the things you've done wrong close the door to heavenly treasures, I ask you: Who would Jesus meet for lunch today? Tell me, who? Deny Himself, or fight His brethren? How does He decide who qualifies to be His fellow being? His companions and followers also carried their own guilt.

Now reflect on how you would respond if God asked you, "What do you want me to do for you?" You can always answer, "I want to love the one who despises me, the one who drives me crazy, the one I wish would be destroyed by fire falling from heaven." That's the person God expects you to focus your love on.

May grace reign! And with its strength, may you overthrow legalism, condemnation, judgment, rejection, death. May grace reign in our lives, in our communities, in our relationships, in our way of approaching the world.

You will always encounter people who don't want to give you space, who will continue to judge you, even if you serve them from the fullness of your heart. However, you will know where you can place your trust because there are signs that overflow with clarity.

Really caring about someone makes all the difference. If they make you wait, give you a thousand tests you didn't know you had to pass, leave your messages "on read," call after the agreed time, answer only what they want, omit details, only show interest in their own issues, ignore what you feel, much less care about what you think, get bored quickly—it's more than clear that they aren't that interested in you. If they were, they'd make everything much easier; they wouldn't fill you with doubt, confuse you, or throw you off balance. It's obvious, but we forget to recognize it in the hope that something will change.

After so many disappointments, if you treat these people the way they treat you, they will shout from the rooftops that you are wicked. I know a cruel wound is inflicted by those who disingenuously say one thing while carrying another thing in their heart. They make you promises, but then do the opposite. That's why we must open the eyes of our spirit and clearly discover those people who only show interest when it's convenient for them, and learn not to condemn people to disappointing us by idealizing them. Because the bad news is that we'll always be disappointed if we continue to think that others will always do what we do for them.

MY GREATEST TALENT IS
TO LIVE WITHOUT RESENTMENT.

Maturing also means to stop insisting, to let go—friendship and relationships are not about begging. Let them go without extinguishing any spark of the love you feel for them in your heart of hearts. Do it precisely so that the bonfire continues to burn without the rocks they throw at it. I don't expect you to become a cold person, I only urge you to hold your warmth for the people who do want to bask in it. Let the others go, but don't let them drag you down.

 ## REMOVE THE STONE

You may find it difficult to determine a course of action when you feel the weight of a condition you've been experiencing since birth.

It's quite common to think that belonging to a certain personality type or lacking a particular intelligence is like a prison sentence, but this is a mistake we must avoid. The reason we engage in self-awareness processes is not to know what prison we're in, but to map out an escape plan.

We can shape even the most complex configurations any way we wish. Leonardo da Vinci is said to have asked Michelangelo how he had sculpted the David to such a superb degree of perfection. The Tuscan genius replied with brilliant eloquence, "I simply carved away everything that was not David."

That is the basic mission we have when we inhale: to be more ourselves every day, to know ourselves well enough to carve away what we decide isn't part of us. Michelangelo chose the figure of the David he wanted. He left us the humble shepherd who consolidated the kingdoms of the world, the one who overthrew Goliath and contemplated the prosperity of his people. Michelangelo didn't want the lustful David, or the one who mourned his beloved Absalom, although he could have made any of these because the marble contained them all.

What will you remove from the marble stone? Use the hierarchy of your principles to define what should go and what should stay. After the progress we've made, knowing yourself better should also give you a clearer picture of how much you can do without. You lack nothing; everything is in the matter of the soul, if you know how to sculpt.

Think of the stone that has shaped you, take the chisel of your desires and sculpt the perfect piece of what you wish to be. Go beyond the physical and imagine the fundamental attributes of what you feel you have enough of to spare; shape it with the hammer of perseverance and dedication. Check out what is missing and ask yourself what part of the stone you need to remove to shape it. You can reduce what you don't want by removing the power you give to what diminishes the essence of who you wish to be. How do you separate vanity and lust from marble? How do you turn the solidity of greed into dust? How do you defuse the power you give to religion, which only serves to alienate you from God?

SO MUCH MATERIAL
FOR SO FEW DREAMERS.

Ezekiel prophesied that we would be able to commit increasingly greater atrocities, to perfect ourselves in resentment. With this sediment of hatred, society has taught us to "love" God. They've inserted religion in their hearts, and to make it fit, they've removed Christ. There lies the tragedy: They love rules more than people; they love traditions more than Christ. It's the vulgar era of an "I" where there is no room for a "we," if that plural doesn't behave as a singular and obedient one. They may spend the day reading the Bible, but not one of its letters is engraved in their hearts.

When I learned to know myself, I removed from the stone that shapes me everything that God doesn't want in it. Anyone could've come out of the crude rock, but I chose to sculpt myself in the likeness of the image that He has for me. He drew those blueprints to perfection in the life of His son. I carved this form that never intends to surrender, for it has been shaped into a dreamer whose work is to make reality a deeper plane, to imagine how to end other people's pain, how to fill empty stomachs, how to heal broken hearts, how to raise dejected spirits. With the chisel that carved me, I wish to tear down walls and build bridges, to confront the irony of pragmatism, to sculpt a dreamer who imagines bombs that explode with caresses, bullets that become healing hands, cells from which the oppressed escape.

In one hand your talents, in the other, the understanding of who you are. With these tools you can shape the image of what you want to be.

Draw yourself. Look at yourself in the once foggy mirror that has been wiped clean throughout these pages. Transcendence is not measured by what they say about you when you leave or when you are dead. You must fully inhale so that your roar is heard by those who will never know you, those you will reach with the love they have for you, with the respect you inspire in them, with the judiciousness of your leadership, with the way you teach them to love.

You could roar by building up your fame, which will surpass your success. But when you build yourself only to triumph over others, you reach the top and have nowhere to go next. Success can be deceiving if it lacks meaning. I prefer dreams, goals. Of course I love to climb mountains and collect peaks, but I also enjoy descending them, because I prefer the life that unfolds in the valley, and walking along its narrow, cobblestone paths.

Up above you were able to laugh at the one who watched you climb, but the height of your faith and dedication can be appreciated more from the ground.

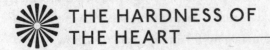

THE HARDNESS OF THE HEART

To shape the stone you must soften it. The rigidity of a callused heart will prevent you from shaping it. And knowing yourself won't do you any good if you view yourself through a sterile lens. Roars find no resonance in the pallor of a numb heart.

THEY CANNOT **SILENCE MY HEART.**

We collect some hardness with time and after accounting for the damage. We live in a world with callused hearts, where love and its virtues are extinguished in the face of the evil forces that drag us to their side, convincing us that it's better to deactivate our sensitivity to avoid further suffering amid so much chaos.

Solomon's wisdom says it with the utmost power: "Happy is the man that feareth always; but he that hardeneth his heart shall fall into mischief" (Proverbs 28:14). Yet we have chosen to keep putting bricks in our chest to increase its rigidity.

Hardness, in its purest sense, refers to resistance that lacks flexibility. Feeling it in many areas of our lives is like opening a rift that keeps us from living in peace. Sometimes we think that having a hard heart is synonymous with strength or wisdom, but deep down we know that although our heart may be made of iron on the outside, on the inside it hurts us all the same. A hard heart is a grueling burden. I understand the wounds that have led us to put on a shell, but that will not prevent it from being broken, because the heart is broken from the soul, not the mind.

A heart filled with God has the ability to absorb energy in great quantities before it is broken. The heart aligned with God can endure the challenges of the molding process and the setbacks that come with it. Only under the pressure exerted in this process can it be completed.

Let's allow Christ to change our heart from stone to flesh, because its hardness brings terrible consequences. Although it may seem like we've temporarily stopped suffering and are better at enduring life, there is a humidity that seeps through our bones and penetrates the foundations of our soul, which breaks us down and makes us bitter.

With time, reason will show us that hardening ourselves didn't do us any favors. On the contrary, insisting on reinforcing our inner hardness in hopes of protecting ourselves will only cause us to lose the joy and happiness we could have chosen to embrace instead. Putting our ego and our vanity above peace and enjoyment entails more than just pride, it's an unacceptable stubbornness considering the brevity of life. Replacing a smile with a scowl to show the world you have a hard soul is a ridiculous, immature, and absurd decision.

What seemed like a victory won by your hardness unravels like a plot uncovering your immense lack of joy. The hard heart forgets how to celebrate, it hides behind the pedestal of superiority and loneliness, preferring to dominate its environment rather than admitting to being vulnerable in the face of love. That is why love is untamed, because it's the only thing that human beings don't know how to handle.

EVERYTHING THAT BREAKS YOUR HEART BUT OPENS YOUR EYES **IS A VICTORY**

The hardness of the heart leads you to live in sadness because it only feeds on what you can give it and closes the door to what others can offer you. You welcome them at the door of your heart, but you never let them in. Don't take this as a recommendation to invite anyone into the chambers of your chest, but as an affirmation that it's better to have someone break your heart than to petrify it by protecting it so much.

You will not be enough for others, until you are enough for yourself.

Without romanticizing pain, I say that only a heart of flesh can feel. When we stop perceiving pain, we distance ourselves from what makes us human, building a wall between what we and the world feel. It separates us from our most beautiful virtues: empathy and mercy. Completely shutting yourself off turns you into someone who punishes without remorse, boasts of not suffering, and lacks the ability to be moved by anything. You applaud your coldness and take pride in it.

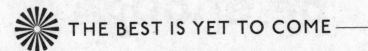 ## THE BEST IS YET TO COME

In this first step you've come across your shortcomings and limitations. I know you've also evaluated your strengths, but we've focused on the former. That's what self-reflection is all about, but we shouldn't dwell on what causes pain.

Punishing yourself will not solve your problems. On the other hand, accepting and acknowledging yourself, and correcting your mistakes, will be your greatest reward. Disrupt your anger without taking it out on anyone. I hope you learn to manage it, not by denying it but by defusing it. Sadness looks back, worry looks around, but faith pushes us to look up. That's why there's something beautiful in Jesus's example. He always taught us how to face pain, not how to avoid it.

I know that suffering and doubts will make you wonder, *What if I fail? What if I don't make it? What if I don't get up?* But God has a habit of choosing the excluded, the discarded, the forgotten, to fill them with greatness, without consulting anyone. So forget all that others have foreshadowed about you. Free yourself from the chains, the expectations, your innermost and private circle. That is healing, which doesn't always mean scars disappear or pain ceases. True fortune lies in not allowing them to control your life. This is the art of wearing your battle wounds well.

Peace will not come when you have everything under absolute control, it will come when you give up having absolute control over everything. The nirvana where we can be perfect doesn't exist. To believe oneself infallible is to deny reality. We must make mistakes and take the next step. If you haven't made a mistake in a long time, you're doing things poorly. You will be dying in place while others will be at the forefront of trying, of expanding in the attempt or in the misstep, because you have to be arrogant to expect to come out on top in pristine conditions. Expecting life to be a thrilling adventure from which we will emerge unscathed isn't funny, it's pathetic.

Every tragedy is an invitation to be reborn. To be reborn as many times as necessary and as many times as we can. There is room for many lives in one life. In a single day, we can determine a new existence. To intervene, to transform, to reinterpret, to eclipse ... all these actions are possible when you don't want to miss anything in your life. There are still skies and seas to cross. We can always rewrite our biography.

HAPPINESS IS A SOPHISTICATED STATE OF DEEP SACRIFICE.

So much wasted talent because of doubts. Throw them away or stomp on them! Otherwise, who can guarantee your success? No one. To be paralyzed is much worse than to fail. Our virtues, talents, gifts wither in hesitation. The hows of life will appear when the dawn of courage dissipates the fog of doubt. Take the plunge! What

DON'T MAKE NOISE,

I'M DREAMING.

an amazing moment when you say, "I'm going to walk!" Creativity is only born when certainties end.

Make sure that the first compliment of the day comes from the mirror—that is how your days, problems, circumstances, people, and emotional disposition will change. We'll still have to work on what we bet on being above all storms. Without a doubt, the best is yet to come, and I'm not only referring to the circumstances, I'm referring to you, acknowledging yourself, recovering from all wounds, loving yourself again, believing in yourself again, multiplying who you are until the end of time.

Here come the victory bells. Cross that arch full of triumphs. Close your eyes and inhale a deep breath. Fill yourself with the oxygen of who you are and prepare to unleash the roar of who you will be.

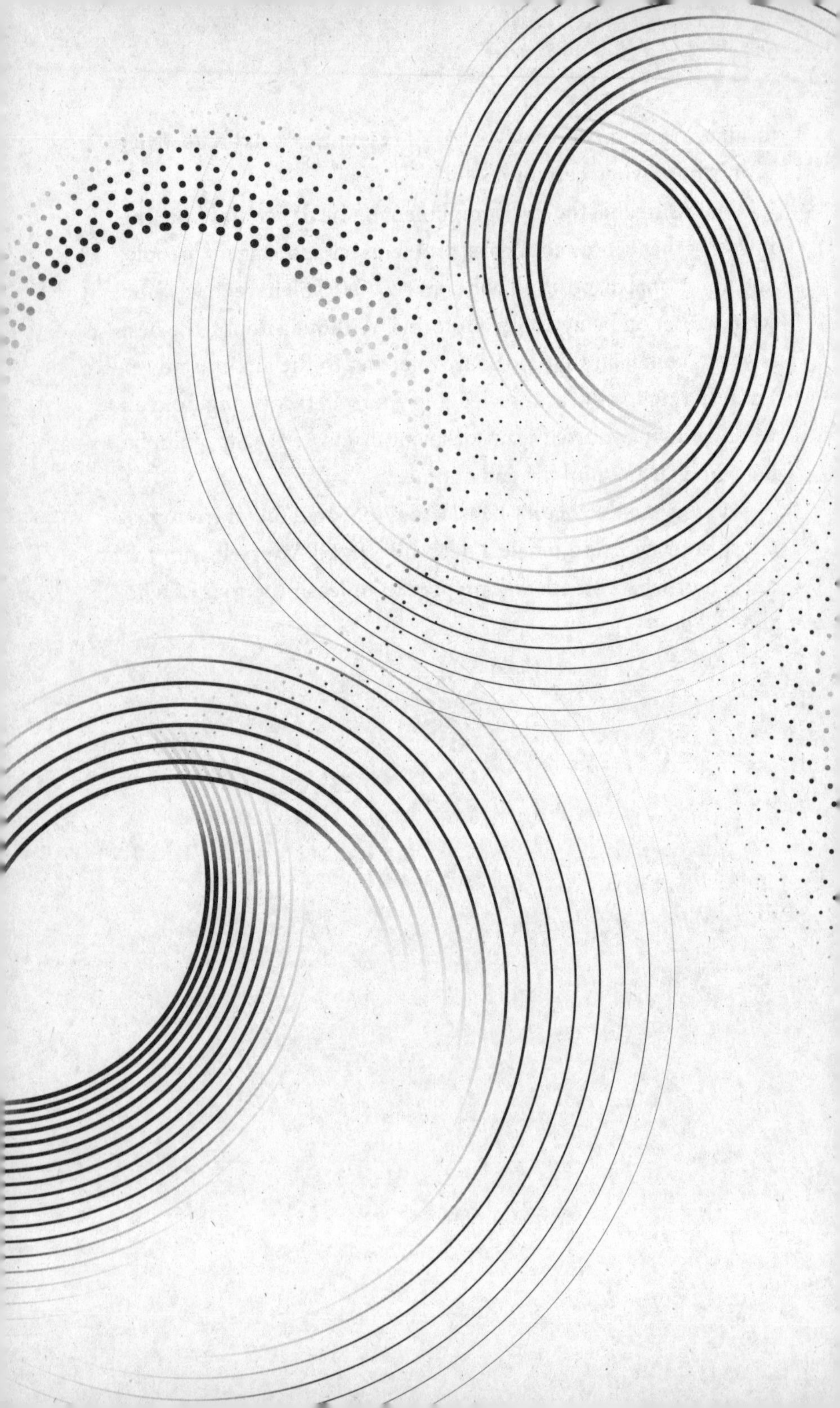

Step Two

INFLAME

To inflame is to intensify your strength and center the prelude of a roar in your throat. It's the moment you decide when and how the bellow that no one expects from you will sound, and you tune the pitch that will break the silence everyone thinks you belong in. This is the moment of stillness where you make wise decisions and plan the sequence of your steps.

To become inflamed is to transform the air by inhaling the wind that moves the mills, not to grind wheat, but to show that we are crazy. It's how we prepare to make mistakes, get up, start again, learn from errors and never forget them, laugh alone, end the silences, be crushed by reality without our knees buckling. We will only do this to raise our hands in gratitude.

After our journey into who we are, which we took in Step One, "Inhale," it's time to process and value all the information we've gathered. Now is the time to be resilient, which has nothing to do with enduring agony, but rather with being like a sling that accumulates immense pressure, on the verge of bursting, and is ready to release the stone that will knock down giants. This is also a time to be still, to let the peace of our mind become dynamic. We can be so ignited by the fever pitch of thought that our ideas end up as smoke and steam without fire. Becoming inflamed is like the soldiers' supper before the call to battle, where we enjoy the wine of ideas before facing them.

This second step in roaring consists of holding in the air to create storms, exploding the crystals of our thoughts, flying flags, making those who dream of ending their lives in one leap acquire the power of flight. Inhale when you feel the downpour and hold in your chest a concentration of air capable of spawning tempests.

 ## THE TEMPEST COLLECTOR

Who am I? I am hoarder of storms, a collector of tempests, a stubborn adversary of downpours. I am the one who one day threw away the maps to redraw them.

I was a man who came from a coastal city, with wooden-beamed houses, fishermen at dawn, and coconuts for soccer balls. My travels led me to strange places, which are my natural habitat. I have ascended from dark valleys along winding paths. I have encountered the forest's winter and the desert's graveyard. I slowly forged my way, accompanied by the cry of crows and the murmur of snakes stirring the fallen leaves. It's not cold in my heart; God's summer melted the glaciers within me.

THE CALM COMES AFTER THE STORM.
DAMN! HOW MANY MORE STORMS ARE THERE?

During the journey, the tide shook my boat several times, but I decided to endure the careening. On land I am a Sherpa who has climbed to the summit, but I don't stop there, I want to cross the mist that lies between the mountains. I am passionate about peaks, but more so about their horizons. I live to be moved by the immensity, by all that I cannot imagine. From the summit you can see new seas, and you must descend to soak in them. I want to be moved to tears by all the sailing.

For me, the sublime isn't only a quality of nature, it's the immense beauty that can only be understood by the senses. Beauty is born of balance, but the sublime surpasses harmony and settles halfway between imagination and reason. Navigating life incites restlessness, disturbance, even terror, and the possibilities of achieving the impossible, touching on the absolute, the transcendent, the abstract, everything that isn't perceived by the physical but is clear to the eyes of the spirit.

I am one who claims an exaltation that aspires to the divine, to the superior, to the extraordinary. I steer between tremors and ecstasy, I am enraptured as I head to the transcendent, to the violent waves that collide between the absurd and the real. I charge ahead, suppressing the vertigo, whether it's my turn to carry the banner on the front line or to defend tooth and nail at the rear guard.

While holding our breath, we must set the strategy to move forward, and to do so we will transform what we have learned about ourselves into the intensity of our roar.

 ## STORMS OF HATRED

When a thunderstorm breaks over the sea, there are two ways to protect ourselves. The first is to get out of the water and seek refuge on the shore; the second is to submerge ourselves in the water as far down as possible because the electric currents will spread over the surface without reaching the depths. The same thing happens with hatred. To protect ourselves from its electric current we can either run away or we can swim down vigorously to reach deeper waters. I always choose the latter.

I have been called ignorant, conceited, a false prophet, a sinner, impious, a fanatic, a snake charmer, a trickster, lukewarm, a conspirer, a charlatan, an executioner. I have been accused of disregarding the Bible and of focusing solely on it; of not being involved enough in politics and of organizing coups d'état; of being a "progressive" and also "right-wing"; superpatriotic and antipatriotic; a pagan and a fundamentalist. I have been called a misogynist and my wife's puppet; they say I'm a traditionalist, but also that I try to destroy institutions; that I always say the same thing and I contradict myself.

Sometimes it's hard to know how to respond to these cases. While letting them go can be tough, it's a mistake to give in to the temptation of those who are just trying to get a reaction from you with their insults. I often wonder why we let these displays of hatred stop us in our tracks, but I'm more concerned about why some people bring their lives to a standstill just to deal with what the people they despise say.

If you have time to humiliate, belittle, slander, hurt, violate, or judge others, you're only showing your enormous fragility disguised as virtuosity. Gaining relevance by destroying others is the most pathetic notoriety to aspire to. Social media is now the Roman Colosseum where thousands crave seeing others perish. It's as if the Inquisition never ended. It just moved to these platforms with millions of executioners who never accomplished anything. Your life stings and annoys them because they don't understand that there are other ways of living, of being, of thinking. So they hide behind their hypocrisy, accusing you of being evil, while they live in total darkness. They pretend to be saints, geniuses, lofty thinkers, but their souls are withered, their hearts are hollow, oozing venom.

> YOU CAN'T STOP AN INSULT FROM HURTING YOUR HEART, **BUT YOU CAN STOP IT FROM DEFINING WHO YOU ARE.**

In this digital world, even when others see you lying broken on the ground, they still want to divvy up what is left of you. But even though they're laughing now, one day that look will be wiped off their faces, because we're all going to have to pay the final bill.

 ## JESUS'S FAME

Behind a lot of hatred is the search for fame, raw and unfiltered, like the goddess with copper lips who spread rumors just for the fun of it.* Some people want a kind of fame that is mistaken for a racket—they want to appear behind the noise as their scandals bring down roofs. They want the flash of fame but aren't interested in seeing the images.

They should look instead for themselves in the example of the man who enjoyed the greatest fame in this world—paradoxically, the humblest man who ever lived. No greater fame has been known than

---

* The Roman goddess Fama (in Greek mythology Feme) was the goddess of rumors, gossip, and fame. She is usually depicted with a trumpet.

that of Jesus. Christ was a celebrity in his day, a true rock star who stopped caravans and whose presence in the world disrupted markets. The word *multitude* appears more than fifty times in the Gospels.

Jesus was acclaimed in the houses of the rich and the poor; those who loved Him and those who wanted to deceive Him fought for His presence. To get closer to Jesus, paralyzed individuals asked their friends to lower them down from the roofs of the houses where He was. And to honor Him, they poured nard perfume on His feet.

He was famous for many things, not just one; for being a rabbi and a false prophet, a healer and a rebel, a savior and a provocateur. Jesus had the fame that came from His deeds, His teachings, His interpretation of the Word, His healings, His forgiveness, His sacrifice, and above all, His love.

Jesus built His fame with truth and kindness, by putting others at the center, and, above all of them, God, His father. He didn't just have a message, He was the message itself, and He communicated it with His life. Everyone wanted to host Him; in the streets they called Him "Lamb of God." The puppet king shouted, "John has risen!"; the legalists said, "It is Elijah." He climbed the mountain, and His prodigies mingled the rich with the peons, the blameless with the sinners. He received a Pharisee who wanted to mock Him, and instead of insulting him, He taught him how to be born again. The devil himself invited Him to his riches, and He who came only to give refused them. He made those who didn't know Him walk, and He didn't even tell them His name.

Jesus built His fame by acknowledging that it wasn't His, that everything He did came from the Father. He sought the endorsement of the sick, the humiliated, the crippled, the blind, the maimed, the prostitutes, the despised. He became famous for them and because of them.

Subtlety is
so beautiful!

Whoever wishes to be famous should follow His example. Fame should come from within, and the outside should only bear witness. If you want fame, ask yourself who would weep with emotion when they see you arrive, why would they pour oils as you walk by, who would celebrate that you left the best wine for last?

If you want fame, ask yourself: Would it come from love?

WHEN LOVE IS SINCERE, IT'S IMPOSSIBLE TO STOP.

Do you want to do something that will break every chain of hatred? Then forgive and love your enemies; none of them expect it. Don't look down on them. Don't back down. Stand firm when they attack, but strike them with pity, knock them off their pedestal, but with the sure blow of love. How can you hate when your heart is full of God? He also wants to redeem those provokers of hate and pain, and He probably wants to do it through you.

 FASTER _____

Digital struggles often involve competing to get more in less time. The culture of levity is obsessed with speed, eliminating duration and turning immediacy into the new standard of living. We are living at the juncture of those who are unwilling to wait: "I want my file to download now," and if it doesn't, "my internet is a disaster." "Swear that I'll have reception in the jungle," they beg. "Tell me there will be a connection underwater and at dinner, when my mother recounts the stories of her youth."

There is no time to contemplate and live in peace. Before

they're satisfied with one pleasure, they're already thinking about the next one. "Look, I've already been outrun by that one, and that other one," they grumble. "What can we do to beat them, how do we beat them?"

In this world, if everything is peaceful, something's wrong. Thirty music singles a year, when artists used to produce an album every two years. "I can't stop making content because people leave. I'd die without their likes," they moan. Creating a lot of garbage and the fact there's hardly any culture doesn't matter. What matters is flooding everything with leftovers, even if the previous post is identical to the next.

The voracious consumption of information makes it impossible to have the serenity needed to think and discern. "So many photos, so many videos, I don't want to close my eyes and miss a single one," they say. "I want it all, even if I don't enjoy anything." If they don't get what they want right away, they feel they've failed. The ego wants more. We don't share the same cell, but we're in the same prison. We've forgotten that direction is more important than speed. We cannot be the generation whose cell phones vibrate more than their hearts. We're addicted to shortcuts. Don't you realize that there is no longer road than a shortcut? Every day, digital mandates are making it harder to just be.

The shock of the unexpected only gives us a flash of pleasure. It's an empire of fake beauty—a mausoleum for aesthetics without any wounds. We're lost in this tide of stimuli and excitements where what matters disappears and the banal becomes evident. The beauty within us has been enslaved by a sensual showcase. The sexualization of the body accompanies the vulgar commercialization of the soul—an identity based on being "desirable," and nothing more. It's a culture that relegates morality to consumption's window display. Failures are not posted. No one wants to show their wounds. Everything must be perfect, spotless, and stretch mark–free. Filters for the face, filters for the belly. Filters for deceit, filters for humiliation.

YOU CAN PUT MAKEUP ON YOUR LIDS,
BUT NEVER ON YOUR EYES.

Today I stand before this truth and flat-out refuse to live under these rules, labels, and molds. For me, sacredness wanders between the beautiful and the terrible. It's the ambivalence of joy and pain. That's why I find everything that's different beautiful, and everything that's the same seems terrible.

Stop wanting to look like others, and pay the price of being. The million-dollar questions are: Who will this society let you be? Will you allow it to tame you, shape you, and shackle you with the weight of its expectations? Will you allow yourself to be defined by the criticism of those who have never spoken to you? Will you let your life be guided by what a few people think of your content? Will you feel sad because of what people who think they know you believe after seeing your image on social media? Will you love your body just because thousands desire it, or will you love it for all it has done for you? Will you hold your breath or will you release your roar?

I refuse to go on like this. There will be days when you'll feel confused and begin to imitate others, but resist, rectify, and relocate. Hundreds of people may wish me ill, but there are millions who wish me peace—one of them is enough for me.

Immediacy has managed to impose its tyranny mostly because we've struggled with the ability to focus. We must remain plugged in, even though we're still lacking energy. We want to be active online, even though we don't move beyond the starting point. We live in search of reception, even though we've lost contact with the real world. We attempt to access the network, even though it's a remote tangled web of loneliness. We count the likes, even though we've forgotten the things we liked the most.

We've invented a metaverse where we're supportive and warm, but in the physical world, we're building a *hikikomori* village, a town populated by hermits. This is largely because we've lost the ability to pay attention, and it's difficult to point what little we have left in the right direction. Many careers, initiatives, and relationships have been affected by the constant pursuit of digital distractions. Let me make one thing clear: Spending a few minutes on social media won't jeopardize our financial and emotional stability—which we'll discuss later as a necessity. The issue arises when we're bombarded with so much noise, we are unable to focus.

 ## DISTRACTED ————————————

Loss of concentration is one of the major problems we've been facing in recent years. Attention deficit disorders are one of the most diagnosed clinical issues in new generations, and this is compounded by excessive distraction. But to unleash the roar in you, it's essential to zero in your attention on the right areas.

IF YOU CAN'T REMEMBER WHERE
YOUR ATTENTION WAS,
**YOU'LL FIND THE ANSWER
IN YOUR RESULTS.**

To pay attention is to understand. Overloading our brain with a thousand irrelevant things wears it out and immerses it in a constant stream of stimuli that prevents us from identifying what we need to see. Being focused is what allows us to identify patterns and anticipate what may happen. This is the only way we can activate our internal translator for the encrypted messages that arrive on the breezes announcing the storm.

When we're distracted, we disconnect from what's important. To start, the word itself delivers the essential message: The Latin root of *distraction* tells us that we're being pulled in the opposite direction. This may seem superficial, but it's of extreme importance because it reveals what's really happening to us: Without attention we can't realize our dreams because we move erratically with no sense of direction.

But distraction doesn't just come from the digital world, it's also found in our thoughts. Fears and imagining possible outcomes are a way to distract ourselves because they drag us down paths we don't want to go. Distractions also prevent us from enjoying the beauty of what we do and the pleasure it brings.

I see a couple sitting at the same table—he's likely checking out the soccer scores, and she's scrolling through the latest news, unchanged since the last time: repeated stories by voices for hire, increasingly less creative, seen hundreds of times. The two people don't lack attention. On the contrary, they have more than enough interest in the insipid void. They talk but do not have a conversation. They dine but do not share. They exist but live trapped in a virtual haze.

As you may have noticed, I've talked about "distraction," but I've never said that people "lose" focus. That doesn't happen. No one loses attention, it just shifts. Our productivity evaporates when the mind prioritizes actions other than the ones we've established. We may even become more focused than usual, but it's on things that progressively divert us from the goals we want to accomplish. Many traffic accidents don't happen because drivers "lost" their attention, but because they diverted it to places, such as their phones or their thoughts, that prevented them from deciphering what was happening outside their vehicle.

If we shift this from the individual to the collective, we see a desolate landscape. Lack of attention is one of the most serious generational diseases. The inability to focus distracts us with the most superficial aspects of ourselves, and then we roll out the red carpet for the worst qualities of humanity. To be unaware of what's going on around us is to regress to one of the darkest times and to redraw the demons that visited our planet a century ago. A gawking society will blindly march toward the worst moments of history: a world ruled by barbarism and widespread menace.

A society that is unable to stay focused on what's important is incapable of analyzing in depth and breadth the things that impact it most directly. Our inability to focus is what has allowed absurd ideas and conspiracy theories to permeate the minds of millions of people, who blindly believe nonsense that rational thought would discard in mere minutes.

LET'S LEARN TO SEE
NOT FROM THE WOUND,
BUT FROM THE SOUL.

Although it may sound strange, knowing how to manage our boredom is a good thing. There are certain techniques worth learning when we find ourselves in situations of constant boredom. We

WHAT DO CLOSED
MINDS GUARD
WITH SUCH PASSION?

feel bored when we don't know what to do with ourselves, so our mind seeks to tune in to an activity that will soothe it. When we're bored, we can't focus on anything we're doing and we can't find an activity that soothes our inner turmoil.

Unfortunately, we often resort to choices that increase the growing dissatisfaction clawing at us from within. These actions don't quench that bonfire because we're focusing our attention on the wrong place. We tend to look outside ourselves, because we find it hard to understand that managing boredom is largely a problem related to *self-control*, something we'll get into more at the beginning of Step Three. That's why you must first accept the source of the issue and stop thinking about it. Then, find an activity that will allow you to regain serenity and calm your nerves: praying, meditating, practicing rhythmic breathing. Once you've gained some stillness, reflect on the benefits of the possible alternatives. What will I learn by reading this? Will I feel better after watching this movie? Will I feel more relaxed playing this? The last and most important step is to find enthusiasm for what you do. Getting out of boredom requires a slight effort.

If you don't approach your boredom as a serious issue, you may end up in unpleasant situations. Your mind's need to find an escape can fling you on a roller coaster of sudden, intense, and absorbing feelings that are unnatural. An all-too-common example is social media reels, which propel you from tenderness to lust in ten seconds, and from hate to devotion ten seconds later. These alternatives create a swamp of immediate gratification that will deny you time to reflect and experience mature emotions. Relying on this sort of distraction will increase your dissatisfaction when doing more uplifting tasks.

Give activities that beautify and nourish your life a chance.

This doesn't mean you need to do things that don't bring you joy or are tedious, but that you decide to get out of boredom by doing things that require effort from within.

Boredom has a strong relationship with the ability to concentrate, which affects our understanding of reality and can give greater momentum to the advancement of lies. In 2018, a Massachusetts Institute of Technology (MIT) study found that fake news spread on Twitter traveled six times faster than real news.[1] When we aren't able to concentrate or take time to reflect, it affects our ability to read properly, to interpret our surroundings correctly, and to be empathetic. So much so that I laughed at those who believed in zombies and ended up agreeing with them. Humanity is suffering a zombie attack . . . and we are the zombies.

Our well-being largely depends on our ability to pay attention to what matters, such as serious social problems, the education of new generations, the destruction of democratic institutions, the abandonment of freedom, and the loss of our spirituality, but above all, to pay attention to ourselves. When we're fully present with our attention, we feel the full force and weight of life.

I hope that becoming aware of the harmful effects of being distracted and not being able to set aside time to think about transcendental issues will increase your interest in regaining control of your attention.

Paying attention to what we do, especially when it comes to our personal objectives, is essential to our effectiveness. Learning to stay focused for a long period of time is one of the most important skills a person must develop to move forward in the conquest of what their soul wants to master. Let's take a closer look at this key topic.

ATTENTION AND FOCUS

I've learned that one of the best ways to stay focused is to forget about how much I do and concentrate instead on how much time I devote my total focus to doing it well. In other words, I want to be as productive as possible during the time I've set aside for a certain task. If I give myself an hour to work on something, I'm not worried about the result, I'm focused on the performance. For example, as I wrote this book, I wasn't worried about how many words I typed in a day, but about how long I was able to stay focused on the objective.

At first, I found it extremely difficult to work this way because I was used to accomplishing tasks that I had written down on a list, not knowing how long they would take or how many I could finish well. Now that I focus on time, I have significantly improved how I set my priorities, because everything fits in my calendar. I do the most important activities more calmly because they're given a fair amount of time. This helps me respond in a more reasonable time frame and I avoid working long hours to meet my deadlines due to backlogged tasks.

On the other hand, I avoid filling my calendar with irrelevant items. This used to be pretty common because I wanted to cross off pending tasks, no matter what they were. Our actions reflect how we measure ourselves, and I measured myself by tasks accomplished, regardless of what they were. Working this way showed me that I was unconsciously doing it to check items off my list to make myself believe that I was getting results. But it only distracted me and handed me small victories, which were useless and ultimately made me give up by creating an illusory sense of progress.

One of the first methods I used to focus my attention on a task for a certain amount of time was the Pomodoro technique.[2] This method is designed to increase the level of efficiency that is lost due to workers' momentary distractions, which may last only a few seconds but make it difficult to refocus for a similar or longer period of time than the distraction. Keep in mind that this methodology is as old as the writer of this book; it was created when many of the devices that now distract us and to which we have an unhealthy attachment didn't exist.

This approach is efficient precisely because of its extreme simplicity. It consists of establishing continuous work sessions interrupted by short mandatory breaks, which also allow you to review your progress. A timer, such as the alarm on your phone, is used to dedicate periods solely to action, without giving too much importance to the outcome at first. The original idea is to set up half-hour phases: twenty-five minutes of work and five of rest. You may think that twenty-five minutes is not enough time to focus, but recent studies show that the attention spans of professionals at work have been reduced to a frighteningly short three minutes.

If you suffer from an attention deficit disorder, do the first exercises in less time. Although twenty-five minutes of focused work may not seem like an excessive amount of effort, I recommend that everyone start with shorter, less demanding periods, and gradually increase them. Starting this practice by exceeding the dosage of the original prescription may cause you to give up before you see the first results, especially if you already have attention issues. Sticking firmly to the time you set for yourself and repeating this routine consistently will strengthen your attention levels.

WHEN YOU CAN'T SLEEP, YOUR APPEARANCE REFLECTS YOUR THOUGHTS.

I use this technique when I'm writing, and sometimes I can go the twenty-five minutes without producing anything I feel is worthwhile, but I still persevere. You may think it's a waste of time, but I prefer to call it discipline. In any case, this technique works for any activity that requires continuous attention. Dedicating yourself to an activity produces results. With practice, you gain flow and efficiency.

As I've gained focus over time, I subject myself to a moderate degree of external noise when writing, which has served to strengthen my concentration. I don't recommend this additional complication if you're just getting started, but as you progress, it will be a useful add-on. It's like when athletes raise the bar to force themselves to jump higher. Those who train with a certain level of distraction perform better. Even when faced with big distractions in real life, their results are usually superior to those of people who work under ideal conditions. In short, a moderate level of tension helps improve focus in complex and unfavorable environments. Concentration can be trained.

Although it may sound strange to you, this is a step that you must also take: You really need to disconnect from the action to get back to it. Resting doesn't mean reviewing what you did or preparing material for what's to come. If you feel a little anxious, using those minutes to meditate would be a good use of your time.

Apply this technique as rigorously as possible. To begin, choose an activity that's important to you and set a shorter period of time than the one suggested by the original exercise. As you master it, gradually increase the duration until you have it under control.

Whenever you have an internal distraction, write it down. By "internal" I don't mean events you can't control, like your cat knocking over a wineglass, but those that come up within you, such as thoughts, concerns, or memories.

Take note of these distractions that come up during the work process and keep track of their frequency and intensity. Analyze why these distractions happen and why they impede your self-control. Aim for them to be less frequent and intense.

Practices such as this one help us create habits that make up for our distraction, but the most important work must be done from within. The most overwhelming distractions arise from within. Turning off your phone notifications isn't enough if you aren't able to disconnect your mind from them. External noise can be controlled, but the most intense work will involve staying focused internally. You can go to a cabin in the Alps to get work done without any electrical equipment or wireless connection, you can run away from the hustle and bustle of people and turn off your social media, but if you don't silence the sirens and alarms that are going off in your mind, you will continue to set your sights on a spot that's far away from your goals.

Put it to the test: Turn off your phone for a long period of time while you're working on a task that you're struggling with, and keep track of the ideas that come to mind and how often you feel the need to see notifications, even if the alarms don't ping. You'll probably start to wonder what you might be missing. Many of the tasks you should've done but forgot will come to mind—the people you didn't call or a pending bank transaction.

How

much

do we die

every

time we

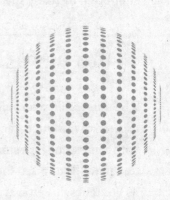

are left

wanting?

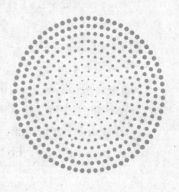

YOU WERE RIGHT IN FRONT OF ME,
AND I DIDN'T KNOW
HOW TO SEE YOU.

For our attention to take the right path, we must calm the storms of thoughts and emotions that cause the most turbulence. Full-blown attention—a concept that books and digital resources refer to as *mindfulness*—is the most efficient alternative to improve our attention. Meditating and performing breathing techniques help us get better results. Although this may sound mysterious or mystical, it's supported by many specialists and academics.

 ## TURBULENCE ————————————

The mind is like a turbulent river. Although it may have pure water, excessive whirlpools can make it look murky, but if we approach it with a glass, collect a small amount of its current, and set the glass down, we'll soon see the opacity begin to decrease and much of its content will settle at the bottom. Breathing is like that crystal glass; it can still your mind to achieve peace.

Some believe that attention is nothing more than a gift, but I'm living proof that it's a skill that can be developed. Certain meditation exercises can effectively calm the internal controls that cause us to get distracted.

When you try it, you'll notice that meditating goes beyond just sitting down and closing your eyes. So, if you've never tried something like this before, start with simple exercises like the following one, but first check out these practical tips that you should keep in mind to get the best out of the exercise:

- Choose a physical space conducive to this practice and, especially at the beginning, free of as many distracting elements as possible.
- Find a comfortable position, but don't let your body lean on anything because that could induce sleep. Do not lean your back on a chair, furniture, or any other type of support.
- Keep your neck and back straight. To help you achieve this, imagine that you're wearing a helmet which, in turn, is being lifted by an invisible rope pulling on your neck and spine.
- Have an anchor to return to when your focus wanders. In this exercise's case, it's your breath.

Once you're ready, close your eyes and start breathing. Choose the rhythm you're comfortable with and start counting your breaths. You can count per breath cycle (in other words, each time you inhale, hold your breath, and exhale would be one cycle) or per action (count each time you inhale and each time you exhale). The first option is more measured and requires a little more attention. Focus all your attention on your breath count. When you reach ten, start again.

You'll suddenly notice thoughts coming in to distract you from your breathing, and it won't be as easy to keep count as described. However, breathing will help you settle the mental dust, and you will be able to hold your focus on a particular point for a longer period of time. Try focusing on the sensations of the breath in your body.

For example, zero in on the movement it causes in the nostrils, on how the air enters the body cold when you inhale and exits warm when you exhale, or on the expansion and contraction of the chest or diaphragm. Choose one of these options and keep your attention fixed on that point without changing the rhythm of the count.

I WAS GOING TO TAKE A BREATH,
BUT I TOOK FIVE.

As you practice this exercise, you'll notice how many thoughts enter the count. At times, your focus will drift. Memories, doubts, thoughts will come to you. . . . Don't be surprised if you lose count of your breaths. Those are the notifications that you can't turn off, the ones that take you from the center to the periphery.

In more advanced stages, these exercises can start to become really complex, and those who engage in them reach states of absolute concentration that can last for hours. Right now, my intention isn't to get you there, but to give you a technique that will improve your ability to focus on what's important.

Many people who have difficulty staying on track find it hard to adopt these practices because they believe they're inefficient for their short attention span. They may also feel that spending twenty minutes a day counting breaths will make them less productive. While it's true that those minutes won't provide you with immediate results, if you don't look for ways to improve your attention, the amount of time you have is trivial. Even if you work twenty-four hours a day, that time won't be fruitful if your mind doesn't stop wandering.

When we feel anxious, our attention retreats to the mind, which is why we lose sight of other factors we should be focusing on. For example, when this happens to high-performance athletes, their mind tends to neglect certain key elements of the competition because they're focused on "calming down." They become so intent on achieving this goal that they neglect the competition's conditions and their inner physical performance, both of which are needed to win.

There are too many temptations ready to distract us. To achieve success, we must prioritize tasks that improve our ability to spend more and better-quality time on the activities necessary to reach our goals. It's not all about hard work. Attention is also needed to enjoy pleasurable moments, appreciate the arts and reading, reflect on our life events.

Enjoying beauty also requires focus. If we're distracted and insist on seeing the world through a screen, we may not notice the beauty that surrounds us. It's like the people who spend a lifetime dreaming of seeing their favorite artist in concert and spend the entire event taking selfies and posting videos on social media. Even to delight in love, enjoy love, and make love, we need to be inflamed with the unifying power of attention.

Attention is related not only to productivity, but also to what we choose to focus on and, consequently, what results we achieve. Some philosophical ideas are based on the concept that what we pay attention to is what we will find. This perspective makes sense beyond how esoteric it may sound. When we focus on certain aspects of our lives, it shows how much we value those areas and how much we prepare for them. But it's mainly a response to how much we neglect to take care of other things. No matter how good we think we are at multitasking, mindfulness is a one-piece puzzle.

We spend so much time reading about other people's lives, while others are writing our own. They're busy doing their *own* thing and we're busy focusing on *them* instead of *ourselves*. When will you take care of yourself? I thought you really wanted to make this happen. When you said you wouldn't accept another day without giving it your all, I thought you weren't just saying it with your mouth but with your guts and with the irrevocable conviction of surpassing yourself and everyone in front of you. Are you still making plans without including yourself in them? Are you still heaving a sigh but not feeling a single drop of sweat on your forehead? Maybe you're just telling yourself you'll do it, but in truth you don't want that life you dream of and say you love so much. When someone loves something, they don't let it go, they fight for it, search for it, seek it, protect it, and don't let anyone take it away from them.

You and I must answer to ourselves. One day we will be held accountable in the eternal for what was given to us, for all that we received for free. And we will have to take into account what we are leaving on this Earth before we depart it, and what will be the return we will bring before the One who asked us to multiply rather than divide or subtract ourselves. I don't want to miss out on anything in my life. I will not let anyone clip my wings, much less pluck them myself.

I NEED TO GET MY INNER CHILD **ON A SWING.**

Another issue that prevents us from focusing is our determination to become multitasking machines. This is a skill we hold in high regard and proudly list on our personal profiles, not realizing that it goes against our brain's nature.

We all multitask, some more skillfully than others, of course. I can listen to the news while I check comments on my social media and write a few lines for my posts, all while eating breakfast.

This becomes more complex with tasks that require a higher level of concentration and mental agility. When we engage in several intellectual activities at once, including those that involve learning, our brain jumps back and forth from one to the other, but it's always a step behind.

Let's say you're writing an email to a key customer. A good relationship with this person is vital to your department's goals. You need to be careful with your words because the text of your email should come across as enthusiastic yet realistic. You need to pay attention to it. As you're writing, your phone lights up to notify you that you've received a message from a person you're interested in, and whom you don't want to keep waiting. (Has that happened to you?)

If we were multitasking organisms, interruptions while writing an email would have no consequence on what we write. But the way our brains work causes our attention to shift from our email to the phone and vice versa. Each time you pivot your focus from one point to another, you're one step behind where you were before because you have to remember how far you've gone and where you left off.

This reconfiguration happens in fractions of a second and will repeat itself with each and every distraction. You may not notice it, so you stand up triumphantly, thinking that you're a total multitasker when in fact your process was inefficient.

The more stuff you do at the same time, the more time you waste. Short interruptions don't improve performance. As a result, spending half an hour on TikTok is more efficient than going in and out of the application thirty times, because these repeated interruptions affect the possibility of finding focus. Human beings are not made to know what to do with the thousands of stimuli they receive today. In just thirty seconds of swiping through our social media, we can go from being moved by a video of a kitten to feeling distressed by a car crash or turned on by a sensual dance; all without discerning, understanding, much less assimilating it. It's a roller coaster of emotions that overwhelms and drowns us. The techniques we've discussed establish clearly delineated periods of focusing and not focusing, reducing interruptions due to jumping between activities and making work time exclusive to one task. If you have any doubts, let me clear them up: Dedicate your working minutes to a specific function. If you have two goals, establish two specific time slots, one for each objective.

SMILING EYES
ARE A MAGNET.

We already know that being focused is essential to igniting the roar within us. This is a crucial task in a world that devotes almost all its efforts to stealing some of our attention. You must exercise discipline until you meet your time blocks. Only then will you be able to move forward. Even paying attention to our rest time is a sign that we're on the right track.

You might think that leisure has no place in a book that wants to exploit your full potential, but the opposite is true. Reflecting on what we can do with our free time is essential, and we'll discuss that next.

 ## THE LAZINESS SIN ——————————

One of the things I can boast about is the use I make of my laziness, that reviled joy from which I have reaped exuberant harvests. While I know the fruits of maintaining a strong willpower, there are mo-

I HAVE ALL THE NOW IN THE WORLD.

ments when it seems impossible to recover from everyday efforts, even when we support ourselves with a healthy diet, adequate sleep, and physical activity. There are times when there is a general strike in our energy and vitality, and we feel out of sync. What is usually relatively easy for us to do becomes an unbearable burden. There are feelings that seem to surpass physical fatigue—I'm talking about a disturbance that settles within us like small traps undermining us from the depths of our being.

There are times when we are inexplicably drained, when we wake up with absolutely no energy. We glide from the bed to the bathroom, from the bathroom to the car, from the car to the office, and we don't know how the hell we managed to get home without having fallen asleep during the day. We also can't figure out why we were so tired in the first place, but the exhaustion is so great that the last thing we want to do is to think.

Although it's a natural, perfectly biological response, when we need to take a break, we think that giving in is reprehensible. We were taught that feeling lazy opens the door to hell. This is not a recent description. One of the most memorable scenes in Dante Alighieri's *Divine Comedy* is his account of the hardships suffered by the idle on the fourth terrace of Purgatory, that place infested with fast-walking souls who feel the urge to make up for the idleness that robbed them of the opportunity to do right. I remember that in this description, these souls were haunted by the what-if shadow and no longer had time to feel or speak. It was a terrible place where unfinished business enslaved us with its reproaches.

In the opinion dictatorship, a large number of influencers attack rest as the worst of vices. They condemn laziness with their posts published shamelessly from some Caribbean beach. Slavers justified their barbarism with the excuse that hard work would improve the health of those they saw as nothing more than merchandise.

I assume you still remember your mother holding your hand when you saw a beggar and using them as an example of what happens to lazy people. Maybe she even gave you a lecture: "That's how you'll end up if you don't study." "That's what will happen to you if you don't do your homework." As if that person's unfortunate outcome didn't involve multiple factors. We've been conditioned to feel bad when we aren't being productive, and we don't always know how to silence that elf who mocks us while we fall apart. We want to find a way to keep it at bay, but our laziness is so great that we've negatively altered all our duties. For some reason, we tend to assume that people in the most miserable conditions are lazy. But few lives require a greater degree of occupation than those who must compensate for oppressive adversities.

IN THESE TIMES OF WAR AND HATRED, MY MOTHER'S ARMS ARE MY TRENCH.

We want to clear our minds, but laziness kills all our endorphins. The body doesn't obey, the mind is tired, and although we do nothing, we are unable to relax. We remember that at some point we were prepared to face conflicts and activities, but lately the energy and physiological bills are so high, we can't afford them.

In a world moving at a speed that makes us retch, it's essential to embrace the subtlety of doing nothing. I receive the most hurtful criticisms when I post a photo of me contemplating the shoreline or enjoying a cigar; it's a constant barrage of criticisms condemning "my laziness," without knowing how I got there. As usual, there's always someone who insists that taking a break or enjoying the moment are actions that are contrary to the teachings of God. They have not yet understood that the Bible must be read, but it must also be lived.

According to an article I recently read, the University of Nevada estimated that distractions caused by mobile apps resulted in an $85 billion loss to the economy. The couple of minutes we spend looking at our phones during work is known as "cyber laziness." But here's a thought: How much would it cost the economy if workers didn't take a couple of minutes off?

While it is costly for people to check their Facebook feed during their coffee break, what would be the price of not being able to do so? These interruptions, if done in moderation as recommended by focus exercises, could actually have an impact on increasing productivity. Pressure and excess are a burden even for those trained in strenuous activities. In the past Olympic Games, several well-known athletes succumbed to the weight of emotions and demands. Diatribes erupted on social media about whether they were allowed to do this, which only added fuel to the fire.

Baseball has had cases of players who lost the ability to throw the ball because of emotional crises. Many therapists have practices full of people suffering from professional burnout, which is marked by somatic and psychological ailments related to the natural pressures of the job, from the workload and the managerial demands to interpersonal relationships.

Some people always work hard and are bursting with energy but this is largely due to the vibe created by elements that give meaning to their work, which we will explore in depth in Step Three when we discuss the concept of purpose.

I LIKE MY MIND
WHEN IT IS UNOCCUPIED.

I recently went on stage in Washington, DC, and gave a lecture of more than three hours, then repeated the effort for five consecutive days in five different cities, covering 2,500 miles. Wake up, travel for hours, go on stage, take care of the people who want to talk to me. Repeat. They are exhausting days that I manage to enjoy as if I were on vacation, largely because I enjoy the support of a close-knit team and the ever-restorative company of my wife.

Many forms of laziness are harmful, but some are necessary. When you don't have the breaks that allow you to recharge yourself emotionally, it's likely you're doing something wrong. If your resting process causes you to feel guilty and makes you more distressed because you're not moving forward with pending issues, then even if you're not doing anything, you're not resting either. You're simply running away.

After accumulating so many tensions, emotions, and thoughts, we can't cope because our vital engines are overheated. Discovering the source of all these harmful emotions and the why of the unconscious tendency to let them pile up will be part of the healing of this wound that looks like laziness. The hard truth in our self-evaluation will lead us to decipher the emotional problem that is hiding behind this strange fatigue and the flood of thoughts that drown us.

 ## DYNAMIC LAZINESS

Without a doubt, too much inaction won't allow us to achieve our goals, but physical, intellectual, and emotional burnout will also eventually cause us to expel our preserved air.

Fighting our emotional stress and learning how to transform it into serenity, peace, joy, and optimism requires a careful cleansing of the mind, which paradoxically demands an enormous amount of energy that we don't have at times, so it's important to find ways to recharge. For instance, I've combined my recharging moments with an endless source of energy: my imagination.

We might think that our imagination can wear us down, but in my case, it replenishes me with power. An unbridled imagination has become my weapon against the laziness that eats away at me. Dreaming without rules, where no one can interrupt me, has helped me reach the most forgotten places of my person.

When I can't take it anymore, I retreat to a place where I can drop my body and let it be. I don't try to force it to do anything, I simply put my hands in my lap, close my eyes, breathe deeply, and begin to see everything my mind suggests to me. Even if I'm flooded with a thousand ideas, I just let them flow. And if one of them excites me, I hold it like a small thread that I begin to pull with the intention of seeing where it takes me. I let myself be carried away by what its colors make me feel, by whether I'm cold or hot, by the fabulous creatures that populate the forests of my mind.

FOR CREATIVE STATES,
DOUBT.

When I lose interest in that feeling, I let the idea fade out and disappear, and the slate is once again clean. I don't mind starting over repeatedly, I just keep breathing deeply and calmly. I let my body do what it knows how to do: heal itself, regulate itself. I don't try to control it, I let it be without restraint, and if it wants to sleep, I sleep. I am committed to leisure as a productive activity, as long as it's my decision. Leisure as a creative state can be highly efficient, since being in a contemplative and low-demand state tends to allow us to find faster and more efficient ways to finish certain tasks. Legend has it that Newton saw that apple fall while leaning against a tree.

However, we've all inevitably succumbed to destructive laziness on more than one occasion. It gives us a short-term state of well-being, which is a product of inaction that leads us not to assume any risks. This opens a direct path to *apathy*, a term that means indifference or absence of feelings, and it abounds in those who tend to leave their life in the hands of their daily moods. If we fall into this cycle, we lose the ability to accept the obligations we establish with ourselves, and fulfilling our inner commitments becomes tortuous.

Listlessness hides the consequences by giving you a worthless placebo. Nowadays, stimuli are so readily available that recovering becomes a feat. We've become used to instant gratification and have lost the ability to truly thrive or enjoy, absorbed by a laziness that instead of energizing us, sinks us deeper.

On the other hand, there's also indolence: doing as little as possible, settling for "it's the thought that counts." If we learn to feel satisfied not only with our successes but also during our attempts, we will be better equipped to keep moving forward until we overcome our own resistance. Some people depend on whether it's cold outside, whether the chair is soft, whether today is game day: external conditions define their efforts. Others blame their family because they didn't set an example, or they don't go to the gym because it's not nearby.

Devoting some time to laziness is healthy only if it's the result of a period of intense effort, not if it comes from the belief that the shortest route is the best. Laziness without tiredness is like bingeing without hunger. This is the attitude of those who throw in the towel because they know it's not their turn to pick it up. They end up seeing life as extremely expensive and every activity as a burden. This can lead them to develop an anxiety disorder or depression. This behavior is not a personality trait; it's not linked to any specific typology or Enneagram type. It has more to do with the acquisition and practice of habits.

I know that sometimes you dedicate yourself to what you want to achieve and that gives you pleasure, but you don't know how to find pleasure in the satisfaction of trying; therefore, reviewing the education we've received can be crucial in figuring out why we take these detours. Overprotection and the rejection of initiative may be their essential source. These attitudes encourage us to flee from what makes us uncomfortable, and that's how we get hung up on effort, without realizing the many benefits it brings us.

HOW DO YOU GIVE
WHAT YOU LACK?

When this attitude of laziness goes beyond the limits of negligence, it becomes dangerous because it modifies our behavior. Instead of creating a break where we find peace, it becomes a mechanism that deprives us of it. Elements of well-being that require dedication and courage—such as economic stability, good physical condition, and the health of personal relationships—begin to slip away.

Although this type of laziness may be pleasurable in the short term, it will have devastating consequences in the future. We will return to this in Step Three when we dive into the idea of self-control. If we allow ourselves to be carried away by these excesses, we give in to the thought that if a goal is far away, it is unattainable, and we lose the desire to pursue it. We don't ap-

I STILL
CAN'T
FIND
REASONS

NOT TO
BE ME.

preciate long-term ideas because they force us to stabilize certain behaviors. We don't really want a goal at all. These attitudes are all about achieving the goal as fast as possible and with as little effort as possible.

Every goal requires effort, which we must also sustain over time. Here are some strategies that have worked for me to reinforce enthusiasm and keep me active:

- Betting on small strides in my life plan
- Honestly reevaluating my goals; it increases motivation
- Finding where I've taken detours from my objectives— this allows me to anticipate and correct myself
- Celebrating efforts I've made and lifting my spirits to avoid contaminated emotional states
- Giving myself proportional rewards
- Getting a good night's sleep and plenty of rest
- Separating the urgent from the important, the necessary, and the priority, based on my convictions
- Focusing on the benefits of doing, not on its difficulties
- Having fun, stimulating myself through activities that guide me toward inspiration
- Attacking first what I don't like to do in the day
- Surrounding myself with content, information, and people that inspire me
- Seeking to be healthy by eating a balanced diet, exercising, and so on
- Avoiding being all-encompassing. Not dividing my internal energy and focus and not imposing on myself

things that, instead of bringing me closer to my life's purpose, distract me and consume my energies

- Constantly challenging myself to improve in a specific area
- Eliminating as many distractions that limit my focus and momentum as possible—that is, anything that isn't a significant addition to my life
- Practicing humility in asking for help and team building
- Setting schedules and learning that maintaining order is not the war I might imagine. There's so much pleasure in moving forward.

Beyond being moved to act by our emotions, we need goals. In other words, we need to get our motivation from the small wins that help us overcome the expected failure. And then we must gain the confidence to keep going and reach a balanced state without falling into a hard line that drives us to the frustration of "I do it because I do it."

In an open discussion, organized by the Economic Club of Washington, DC, Jeff Bezos, founder and former CEO of Amazon, revealed that one of the formulas he used to improve his productivity was to sleep more and better.[3] This digital business pioneer mentioned that rest allowed him to make better decisions and that most of his work consisted of executing this action appropriately.

SOMETIMES
THE FEAR OF SUCCESS
PREVENTS ME FROM SLEEPING.

While some "opinion leaders" make fun of people who "sleep too much," there are those of us who enjoy more and better productive hours when we sleep well and, like Bezos, believe that making good decisions is our most important daily task.

 ## THE DECISION RECIPE

Life is a series of endless decisions. Some of them sneak in unnoticed but can have an impact on the rest of our days. If you look up how many decisions we make in a day, you'll find that it's about forty per minute. Obviously, any movement involves a small decision, but many of these are made almost automatically. Regardless of how accurate that number is, some of these decisions have consequences that will haunt us for years, some for the rest of our lives. Whom did I marry? Why didn't I emigrate? Why did I partner with that person? Why was I such a coward?

When we do self-awareness exercises, such as those in Step One, we have to understand the reason behind many of the decisions that plague us. When we know what we're really after, we get why we lean one way or the other.

Given that decisions can play such a determining role in our lives, we need to analyze how we arrive at them and be willing to unlearn old habits. Many of our mistakes are due to the unconscious repetition of mental patterns that we must strive to abandon. Start with the intention of introducing a new way of looking at the facts, but aim to develop new habits as a result.

Like in a cooking recipe, decision-making is made up of a list of ingredients, procedures, techniques, and equipment, but no matter how much you control the method, the outcome will be influenced by the quality of the ingredients, external conditions, and the chef's previous knowledge. We will be able to fix some of these elements, others will need to be offset, and then there will be those that we must accept as part of the process.

Each day begins with the transcendent decision to close your eyes again or to get up and live your day. I know some of these choices may not be made with complete freedom, but they are still decisions. In my book, *Las trampas del miedo*, I mention that the brain is lazy. Spoiler alert: This has nothing to do with your intelligence. The brain looks for ways to process information using as little energy as possible, so it resorts to shortcuts and automations to make simple decisions, like choosing the best route from home to work. The problem is that these same mental patterns are activated when the time comes to make important decisions that can redefine the course of your life.

Decision-making is a complex process that involves several factors: Some are primary and within your control while others are secondary and come from the environment, which cannot be changed immediately. However, using a culinary analogy, if you don't have the right ingredients, it doesn't matter how precise you are with the process. Likewise, even if you use the finest ingredients, they will lose all their attributes if you don't follow the right steps. Assuming this is clear, let's revisit the cooking example to create something perfect.

CONDEMN YOURSELF
TO THE TRIUMPH
OF YOUR PASSIONS.

The ingredients are basically what you bring to the table to make decisions. If you use bad sources to inform yourself, you'll get results that are very different from what you expected. Recently, millions of people feel more comfortable with what they read on an anonymous social media account than with what a professional journalist has written in an independent publication. The same goes for individual appraisals: Some will readily eat up what they've prepared with gossip and entanglements, hoping that it will nourish them. Statistical manipulation and the surgical use of out-of-context situations raise clouds of dust that obscure the glass through which our perception of reality is filtered. And no matter how hard we try, it will remain just that: a perception.

Finding the right ingredients has a lot to do with where we look for them. Another key aspect involves the questions we ask ourselves: We will get different answers depending on what we question. The quality of what we add to the pan will also be related to how we use language. Several studies have shown that when we ask the same question from different perspectives, the answers will vary.

The way we ask questions has as much impact on the answers as the truth itself. For example, after a medical checkup, if the doctor tells us that we need surgery but we "shouldn't worry" because 90 percent of the patients leave the operating room without any problems, we will have a very different response than if the doctor tells us that we must "unfortunately" undergo a surgery where 10 percent of the patients may suffer complications. They are the same ingredients, but not the same recipe. Usually we will change our minds in a situation where we see a greater possibility of losing than winning, even though the chances are the same. Many studies reveal that we may think twice before jumping on opportunities, but we run away from risks at first sight.

I insist that the biggest problem with decision-making is the ingredients we add to the recipe. Many of them are stale because of our prejudices. It's only natural for us to discard information that contradicts our core beliefs and to highlight what reaffirms them.

It's like seasoning; although everyone has the same information, each of us adds more of what we like to the final recipe, even if it's unnecessary.

PREPARE THE INGREDIENTS ——

The only way to know how much of each ingredient we should add to the decision recipe is to measure them. If you are an overcautious person, you know all your recipes will be a little too prudent. On the other hand, if you like to take risks, you may be a little too bold. That's why it's so important to find a stable recipe and identify what we're adding too little or too much of, so that we can make up for it at the end of the day and reach a balanced decision.

ARE YOU LISTENING WITH ANYTHING OTHER **THAN YOUR EARS?**

Our brain works like a decision-making factory, but the outcomes depend on how we program these decisions. Here's a simple tool that you can use in other concrete and abstract areas. This recipe is designed to help you decide between different options and to minimize the impact of the subjective dimension. Since it's schematic and concrete, one of its key advantages is that it reveals the biases operating in the decision-making processor within you.

Before using the tool, I want you to be aware that the "best option" doesn't exist. Each individual situation is different, and our

CONFIDENCE

ISN'T
REACHED
WITH
SHORTCUTS.

searches are conditioned by the parameters we set according to our interests. This may seem obvious, but experience shows that many mistakes happen precisely because we make decisions based on criteria that aren't optimal for our interests.

Following is an example of how your internal configuration works. Let's say you want to buy a computer and hope to get the best price-to-performance ratio available. First off, that choice depends only on what you want. In my case, the ideal choice for writing this book isn't the same as the one for designing its cover, so the factors to be evaluated must be different. Consequently, we will get different results depending on the recipe we use, even though the assessed factors are exactly the same. This applies to choosing a house, a business, a company, a candidate, and even to certain personal decisions. In the example we've chosen, there are dozens of different factors that come into play, but some of them add so little flavor to the final outcome that it would be pointless to use them, much less make them part of the hierarchy.

The first step in the process is to list the criteria and select only those that have a direct impact on what you want to achieve. As I said earlier, the perfect relationship is built by the needs that everyone wants to satisfy. For this example, I'll use five ingredients:

- Brand
- Price
- Monitor size
- Processor
- Memory

Each person will play around with the measurements that suit them. If your intention is to have a computer to reproduce or create designs, the graphics card should be added to this equation. If you travel a lot and spend a good part of your time in airport lounges, then battery life is a key element. The specifics never end. However, if there's an existing criterion you don't think is that important, you shouldn't include it because it'll just slow down the calculations without adding much.

You may think that I'm contradicting myself because the price-to-benefit ratio has subjective criteria, and a while ago I said that we must try to eliminate subjectivity from decisions. And yes, you hit the nail on the head: Every decision will always have elements of subjectivity, so you must be the one who's in control of them, not the other way around. It's better to introduce these aspects—such as design, brand, or prestige—and know that they are part of the game, than to introduce variables that aren't important to you.

I AM MORE THAN **ENOUGH TO BE ME.**

After choosing the list of ingredients, let's move on to review the options. Let's say there are five computers on the market and you want to see which one works best for you. I invite you to make a chart like the one below and rate each option:

	Option 1	Option 2	Option 3	Option 4	Option 5
Brand					
Price					
Monitor Size					
Processor					
Memory					

This exercise can be done many ways, but I recommend using a numerical scale to rate your criteria, such as from 1 to 5, no matter how many options you may have. You should use the same rating system whether you're reviewing three houses or twelve cars. You'll be reviewing basic elements, such as price and the amount of memory, and more complex ones, such as the brand. For the subjective elements, like the brand, there are several rating options:

- Use an independent ranking system: There are many online sites that review and rate brands.
- Consult with experts: Here you'd be using several arbitrary judgments to create a rating.
- Eliminate it: If you can't establish a comparison or if the element at stake can't be determined, then you should think twice before using it. If it has weight, you should be able to assign a value to it.

Following is an example of a completed chart showing the rate assigned to each criterion in the different options.

	Option 1	Option 2	Option 3	Option 4	Option 5
Brand	5	4	4	3	3
Price	4	4	2	4	5
Monitor Size	4	5	5	3	2
Processor	5	3	3	4	3
Memory	2	3	4	4	5

Once you've completed the entire chart, a question will come up: How much of each ingredient should you add to get what you want? It's time to start writing the recipe. Usually a recipe takes more of some ingredients than others, hence the seasoning. A simple way to start figuring out how to assign measurements is to divide 100 percent by your number of criteria. In our case, there are five, so the balance would be 20 percent. Obviously, if we assign this measurement to all ingredients equally, none will outweigh the other, which is not impossible, but quite unlikely in practice. This isn't bad, but it will rarely work. The idea is to give a higher percentage to the most important things, while making sure the total is always 100 percent.

The assignment of the percentage values is subjective, so the result may vary from one person to another—exactly what we're looking for. For this example, I will use these measurements for the different criteria:

	Dollars
Brand	5%
Price	30%
Monitor Size	15%
Processor	40%
Memory	10%

The next step is to multiply each criterion's rating by the assigned measurement, so we can assign measurements to the attributes.

Let's use the brand as an example. As we saw, option 1 had a score of 5 points for this criterion. Given that the measurement we assigned that criterion was 5 percent, we multiply the score by the measurement (5 × 5 percent), and get a result of 0.25 percent.

I'M NOT ALWAYS SURE WHERE I'M GOING,
BUT I KNOW EXACTLY
WHERE I DON'T WANT TO RETURN.

Repeat this exercise for each of the elements you're going to review and record the results in a chart like the following one, which, as you can see, has a total of the results per option in the last row.

	Option 1	Option 2	Option 3	Option 4	Option 5
Brand	0.25	0.2	0.2	0.15	0.15
Price	1.2	1.2	0.6	1.2	1.5
Monitor Size	0.6	0.75	0.75	0.45	0.3
Processor	2	1.2	1.2	1.6	1.2
Memory	0.2	0.3	0.4	0.4	0.5
TOTAL	4.25	3.65	3.15	3.8	3.65

As you can see, the most qualified computer is the one in option 1. Using the same inputs, but with another recipe, the result would be different, but both would be perfectly valid. This method makes sure that variables you don't control or that aren't relevant don't affect the result.

EQUIPMENT

If you find using decimals and percentages too complex, here's another strategy for decision-making, which focuses on the criteria we use or discard when making a decision. Let's go back to the previous exercise and eliminate the excessive calculations—we'll cook with fewer containers.

This time, instead of assigning a percentage to each criterion, you will organize the list of criteria in order of importance. Once you have defined this, start with the most important criterion for you, review which options have the best rating for that criterion, and select only the options that have been rated as "good" or "very good" (if using the numerical scale, this would correspond to 4 or 5, respectively). Eliminate the rest.

SUCCESS IS TRUSTING SOMEONE
AND BEING RIGHT.

Continue with the second most important criterion and review the scores of those options. Once again, eliminate the options that have the lowest scores. Continue doing this exercise with the remaining criteria until you have only one option left: the chosen one.

This way you'll get an answer without doing any calculations. Just prioritize your list and eliminate the options that were poorly scored, in order of importance. The advantage of following this method is that you advance faster; however, you may move away from the "best" solution in some cases, the one that we build with the most metrics. I suggest you choose the first method for decisions that require more reflection and the second, faster one for simpler options.

Now let's move away from the amount of each ingredient in the recipe and explore the second essential component of decision-making: the climate.

CLIMATE/CONTEXT ANALYSIS

The preparation of our decisions is also affected by external conditions. The daily situations we experience shift our perception of certain elements. In the computer example, specific events, such as a bad report on the economy, can change the importance we give to a certain criterion and lead us to make a totally different decision. News, stories, everyday occurrences that we have never related to the subject can trigger or modify our decision.

As I write this book, for example, the world is experiencing an energy crisis. If you were to buy a car right now, perhaps "performance" would become an important criterion you had never thought about.

The climate also has a bearing on social decisions. A clear example can be found in politics: Your rating of a problem like insecurity will increase if you're the victim of a mugging or a shocking public event takes place days before an election. Knowing this is important because your decision will be largely influenced by the disproportionate value placed on that aspect.

Therefore, you should be aware of this reality and try to regulate the way in which the climate affects you when you have to make a decision, because the result may be influenced by an event that's been blown out of proportion and reduced the weight you give to the really important elements. Being well informed minimizes the impact of isolated events on our assessment of reality.

The key is to continue working on building your own intelligent decision-making method. The way we obtain information to assess

The
void
is
enormous
if
you
only
notice
what
you
don't
have.

the situation is critical here, especially at a time when there is so much access to manipulated and inefficient data. Rarely have we been subjected to so much fraud, lies, and misrepresentation as during the COVID-19 pandemic, and the outcome was not the best.

MY APOLOGIES TO INTUITION; I IGNORED IT.

In addition to the external climate, meaning the environment around you, there is also an internal climate created by the emotions you experience when making a decision. It's very similar to what happens to Tita in Laura Esquivel's novel *Like Water for Chocolate*, who imbued the food she prepared with the emotions she experienced while cooking.

We can have top-quality ingredients and the best techniques, but our emotions will have an incredibly relevant impact on the final dish we set on the table. We need to make up for this. Our grandmothers always said we should avoid making decisions with a "hot head." If I'm sad, I may see things differently than if I'm happy, but the issue is much more complex than that, and we need to talk about it. Conventional wisdom suggests separating thoughts from feelings, when one is actually shaped by the chisel of the other. The only thing we can do to minimize the effect of those "hot" or "cold" heads is to understand that the decisions we make with extreme joy or sadness will never be the best examples.

Extreme emotions will tend to produce extreme decisions, regardless of whether they're positive or negative. An excessively cheerful person will tend to make mistakes similar to those who feel anger or seek revenge. Knowing the emotional states from which we operate is essential because they will creep into our decisions.

Once you've followed the recipe's step-by-step process—picking top-quality ingredients, meticulously following the preparation instructions, and making sure there's a favorable climate for everything to work—you still need to like the result of what you've prepared: The time has come to listen to yourself because that's where you'll find the missing data.

INVISIBLE FACTORS

We've done an exercise to reduce subjectivity in some decisions. Then we added the effects of the weight we give to information and analyzed how our emotions come into play. But we've left out other criteria that are related to what we can't control ourselves, although we can look for ways to do so. Sometimes, no matter how much math we use, the key lies in knowing ourselves better, as we discussed in Step One.

> TO BE LISTENED TO
> **WITHOUT JUDGMENT**
> IS BEAUTIFUL.

Doing these exercises helps us make more balanced decisions, but there's another benefit that's not always discussed: It forces us to be honest about what we want and why.

The following anecdote helped me understand this benefit. Shortly after studying these decision-making methods, and as if he'd wanted to test me, my brother told me he wanted to buy a car. I felt happy. It was as if I could try out a new toy. I convinced him to use a model like the one we reviewed a few pages earlier. After a fairly meticulous search for information, he chose eight criteria for four vehicle models and carefully reviewed them. When it came time to rate them, one of the cars was the clear winner. "No way," he said. "Let's do it again." We did it again after adjusting the values. The winning car came out on top again, but my brother was still suspicious.

He wanted another result. His ego had already made a choice and he only needed the calculations to confirm it. This doesn't mean the calculation model was wrong. My brother just never took into account the factors that were relevant to his personal configuration. He didn't add them to the equation, and he didn't reveal them either: prestige, design, affinity, and others that perhaps he was unable to recognize—or never wanted to admit—such as symbols of power in his social environment, nostalgia, or vanity. That's why it's important to know if what we've added to the equation responds to our most sincere desires. When buying a car, I don't think many people add "I want everyone to notice me when I drive by" or "I want to look like Brad Pitt" to the equation, yet that doesn't mean these things don't have an impact when it comes to assessing the vehicles.

Tools such as these serve to minimize, never avoid, subjective bias, or at least give us the courage to admit to it. It's even harder to isolate decision-making from personal issues, such as relationships, entrepreneurship, or your college major. These must also be accounted for.

It may be that our inability to draw conclusions has to do with our inability to accept the decisions we make. This may be related to the distance that exists between what we want and what we consider adequate. Can I pay the consequences of the decision model I have chosen? This is the big question we face when we must weigh our priorities. Weighing each criterion can be a struggle between what is desired and what is right, between what we expect of ourselves and what others expect of us. Resolving this struggle is a process that precedes any plan. Disregarding the importance of these aspects may lead to dissatisfaction with whatever results we get.

But not every important decision is ours to make. Sometimes we care about the decisions made by others whom we can influence. To roar, we need the echo of those who can hear us and will consider our ideas; hence the importance of knowing how to influence others.

 ## RESONANCE

The need to persuade is innate. From a very early age, we use all available resources to persuade others to react in the way we want them to. Among our first acts are crying, moaning, or knocking things over to get a reaction from our parents. You have that ability, but you may have lost a little confidence to make it work.

Knowing how to persuade is not about going through life maliciously manipulating people to always act in your best interest. It has to do with maximizing the mechanisms that allow you to accentuate your voice. The value of influence in business and personal relationships will come to mind, but it's also important in areas you may never have dared to enter, such as conceptual fields or spirituality.

We must abandon the idea that persuasion is getting others to do our bidding even when they don't want to. It's so much more than that. Rather than using these tactics to sell a used car, they can become a key to changing attitudes or achieving cohesion, because learning to influence others also allows us to learn more about their ideas and to increase our own tolerance and that of those around us.

YOU NEVER KNOW WHAT BUTTONS CERTAIN WORDS WILL PUSH.

Influencing is not a one-person job; it's made possible through interaction. We have all the resources at our disposal to help our counterpart reach their conclusion. We will not always succeed in imposing our vision; it wouldn't be good for anyone if that were to happen. Having resources to persuade improves the quality of our communication, allows our ideas to resonate, and increases the power they have to influence decisions. When your ideas are understood, valued, and considered, the benefits are immediate.

We're often vulnerable to someone trying to sell us something. Fortunately, we don't succumb to every detergent or coffee commercial we see. First, we are not the target of the vast majority of the products we are exposed to; only a few messages are geared to our profile or our way of thinking. But even when we're the focus of certain products, some will get our consent and some will not. At the end of the day, we will only succumb to buying a certain number of the hundred products that try to seduce us.

In the face of effective influence, no one feels that they've lost control because everyone has been able to consider their options and come to a conclusion without unnecessary pressure. But manipulation is nearby—an inhospitable, oppressive, dictatorial territory. We know we are facing manipulation when there is only one clear winner. It may sneak in undetected, but it will not take long to be discovered: Manipulation always hides between two evil choices. It arises from the contamination of the soul. It is a raptorial, emotional plunder. It sows weeds that only serve to poison the soil.

Certain psychological techniques can convince young people to join hate groups, girls that their only asset is their body, pensioners to invest their life's efforts in a hollow pyramid. The power of manipulation is immense. Likewise, it has been used for good, to call for peace and promote solidarity. Therefore, it's important to know when we're facing mind games that seek to alter our decisions. Nowhere has this been more skillfully played out than in sales tactics. These include transactions of products and services, and also the dissemination of ideologies and dogmatic thoughts.

When we try to influence others, there are several factors we must monitor. To better understand this, let's simplify it as a model and look at its most relevant components. First, there are those who are trying to cause a reaction, that is, those who want to persuade. Let's call the people they want to convince the *target*. Only a specific group of them will receive the message. Communication happens through a *method*, which produces *responses*. All these factors are enclosed within a set of circumstances that will affect the outcome. For example, messages of hate and violence elicit one response in times of prosperity and another entirely different one in times of economic and social crises, even when the messenger, their targets, and the method remain the same. As you can see, this is related to the decision recipe model: same ingredients but different climates during the preparation.

THANK YOU TO THOSE
WHO TEACH ME WHAT
I DON'T WANT FOR MYSELF.

I THINK YOUR
"HUMBLE"
POINT OF VIEW
IS MYOPIC.

The reason for this analysis is to discover the factors that can help us become more persuasive while simultaneously protecting ourselves when we're on the receiving end of persuasion. Throughout this process, we will always have absolute control over one of these criteria: the messenger, because that person is us and how others perceive us.

 ## INFLUENCE MODEL

As we've seen, two people can get different results from a similar target, even when using the same method. Several factors can affect these results. A significant one is the person's likability. We're more inclined to follow people we find attractive. The teachings of the Koran say, "God is beautiful and loves the beautiful." Although God loves everything, we sometimes use His name to describe behaviors that are entirely human. This beauty that Islam mentions largely describes patterns of how we, not God, have a predilection for the beautiful. This refers not only to physical attractiveness, but also to charm, position, and any other criteria that enhance the message bearer's appeal. Our species is inclined to please the people it likes the most.

There are two fundamental conditions for increasing this attractiveness: first, looking like the kind of person the target wants to be, and second, being someone they can relate to through shared similarities. The chances of getting a positive response increase if the request comes from a person with whom we have developed an affinity. In short, you should always seek that genuine connection with those you wish to conquer, a method that modern tyrants and coercive cult leaders have unfortunately learned quite well.

The idea is to establish a relevant starting point, such as musical taste, a name, or a hometown. Then it would be helpful to pay attention to other things you have in common and highlight them. One way of increasing this sense of similarity is through imitation, carefully repeating the words, gestures, or actions of the person with whom we are interacting. This exercise increases affinity levels, which in turn increases sincere likability and the chances of succeeding.

It should also be noted that a positive image is strengthened by demonstrating facts, credibility, authority, and knowledge. And this is something that can't be built without effort and can't be imitated. Our suggestion must also respond to the interests of those we wish to persuade; there must be something for them to gain. It's not about offering a bribe or igniting a smoke bomb, it's about allowing the decision to happen naturally, without coercion. Sometimes the benefit to the target isn't too clear. That's when indecision sets in, which often leads to a mental block. In this case, the best thing to do is to find support from people who have the same perspective you want to promote.

UNTIE THE KNOTS
WITH CONFIDENCE'S FINGERS.

In China, the expression "three men make a tiger" refers to the impact of receiving concrete support from three sources. Beyond Eastern wisdom, there are studies that quantify the persuasive impact of introducing a third source. The Chinese expression comes from the story of a wise counselor whom the emperor sent on a journey far from the palace. Knowing that gossip and intrigue would rain down from his adversaries upon his departure, he told the emperor before he left to beware of such remarks. The royal insisted he wouldn't believe anyone who spoke ill of his beloved adviser, but the counselor asked him, "If someone told you that there was a tiger in the palace, would you believe them?" The emperor bluntly said no. "And if, along with this messenger, another one came along and said that he had seen a tiger, would you believe him?" The emperor insisted that he would not. "Suppose that before these two messengers leave the room, a third one arrives, alarmed, and says that he's seen a tiger. Would you believe him?" The emperor hesitated and said, "I'd think that, for some unexpected reason, a tiger had escaped from captivity and entered the palace." The sage stood looking at him and said, "See, Your Majesty, three men make a tiger. The same thing will happen to the lies they tell you about me when I leave. Ask me about anything they tell you about me."

The saddest evidence of the power of other people's opinions doesn't lie in traditional psychological knowledge but in the crude reality of the behavior of societies mobilized by masses of people enraged and alienated by the most absurd ideologies. Even the best families can experience this, as proven by the German experience almost a century ago.

Ironically, a Polish Jew came up with one of the most eloquent investigations to prove how the collective's opinion alters our reasoning. In the 1950s, Solomon Asch conducted a research project in which he invited groups of students to take a test. He had them enter a room full of other "participants," who were no more than the researcher's minions. The recruits were exposed to a series of figures containing lines of different lengths. The idea was that each participant, following a pre-established order, would indicate which of the lines was the longest. One after another, the minions provided wrong answers, and with this group tendency, the answers of the research subjects changed. The experiment's results demonstrated how social pressure can impact our perception of reality.[4]

If one of the researcher's minions gave a deliberately wrong answer, the impact on the research subjects was minimal, but this influence increased significantly when the number reached three or more "wrong" answers. That's the thing: Three opinions can make a tiger appear.

Often the collective opinion is formed spontaneously and carries us along. But other times mobilizations are the result of carefully planned strategies that cause a snowball effect in which a few convince others, and this becomes an avalanche of lies to the maximum extreme.

Asch's research reveals that a totally rational person can be pressured to deviate from their levelheaded behavior. The results are compelling in demonstrating that group reactions can lead to behavior that is inappropriate or out of touch with reality.

SOMETIMES WE DON'T FALL INTO SADNESS, SOMETIMES WE'RE PUSHED.

This is why companies make such an effort to show how many followers they have. It's a common practice in nightclubs to create conditions to gather a lot of people at the venue's entrance, and thus create the idea that there's a crowd eager to get in, even though there is room inside for many more customers than those waiting outside. In politics there's a race to see which candidate can get the largest turnout at their rallies, which also becomes a perception struggle. "The most read book" and "the most visited park" are typical messages that don't focus on intrinsic attributes, but on developing the idea that if many people like it, it must be excellent.

I gave him
my heart
because he
offered me
his soul.

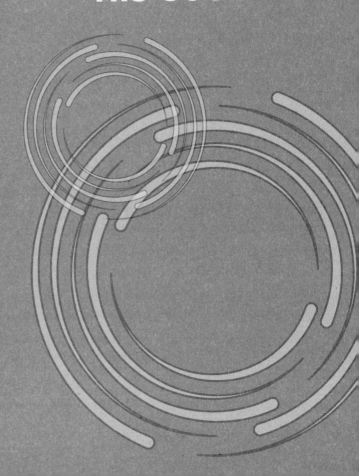

One of the panhandlers in my neighborhood always starts the day with his basket half-full. And he's the one who gets the most money. You might think the empty basket would earn him more points because people would feel bad for him. Well, no. Showing money in the basket is a way of communicating that other people are giving to him, that it's a norm, that it's approved. The behavior of others produces this reaction. That may be why influencers often buy fake followers.

While it only takes three people to make a tiger, the word of a powerful person can make a herd appear. Someone in a position of authority will have a similar effect to that of a group, except that now we're talking about just one person. As always, authority will be relative to the point of comparison. For example, a doctor friend may help us convince our partner to change some of their eating habits, or an accountant convince them to stop wasting money. People who exercise specific leadership, such as our bosses or those who manage a process we're engaged in, also enjoy this power. Authority is reinforced by symbols of power, such as coats and uniforms. This situation exacerbates the risks caused when certain leaders with vast resources sway public opinion in directions they know are false.

Just as approval is a resource, so is authority, which is why recommendations from people who are an authority in their field are so sought after.

 ## THE GIFT OF MANIPULATION —

One of the greatest contributions regarding influence was the work of Robert Cialdini, a professor of psychology and marketing who did extensive research on major sales methods and why some of them are so effective. Cialdini's work has had great impact not only in the academic world—in which he earned induction into the American Academy of Sciences—but also in the publishing world, where his books have become bestsellers, precisely because they've turned into guides for millions of salespeople around the world.

WHEN WORDS BEGIN TO WEAR THIN, FACTS BEGIN TO TALK.

One of the tactics that has had the greatest impact on me bears the name of a beautiful gesture, although in this case it's not spontaneous: reciprocity. In his research, Cialdini found that there's a natural tendency to reciprocate something that has been done for us.[5] Let's see how it works so that we can identify when we might want to use this resource and know if our decisions are being influenced by this.

Reciprocity in sales often consists of something being given with the intention of paving the way to getting something in return. Preachers of certain faiths have become famous for giving gifts such as flowers, books, or stamps to get people to give them at least a few minutes of their time. After receiving this type of gift, the walls that people usually put up come down and they stop to listen. This practice was later copied by marketers, especially to promote services and subscriptions, and often goes unnoticed, like when you're at a restaurant with friends and the waiter says, "Here's an extra plate of nachos, but don't worry, this one's on the house." I'm sure he earned himself a good tip. The tip is a reciprocal gesture.

This information is meant to help you identify when you're being influenced, but also to show you why these practices are so effective and difficult to recognize. Two necessary criteria must be met:

- The gift needs to be sincere. This rules out a good chunk of the "gifts" we receive, full of ads. We don't hesitate to throw those away and they lose all validity.
- The gift needs to be moderate, because disproportion is a red flag. It must be a gesture, not bait. An excessive offering may lead us to think that receiving it comes with a cost. It won't go unnoticed.

By being aware of this practice, you can be more vigilant, though not necessarily immune to it. To avoid falling into these traps, it's always advisable to review the reasons behind why you decide to buy, contribute, or surrender your position. You must know if your decisions are being affected by external favors. If so, you must clearly establish your positions and not change them in the face of presumed benefits received from the opposing party.

Sometimes the "gift" is something intangible or has no economic value, such as a concession. For example, giving in to someone else's wishes. This concession may only be granted in order to give the person granting it influence or an advantage of some other kind.

In short, we have several social mechanisms to influence others in a positive way: consensus, likability, and reciprocity. Persuasion is the step prior to the roar because it allows your ideas to reach a safe harbor.

COMMUNICATION TODAY
IS A MINEFIELD.

The possibility of developing skills so that our ideas gain resonance prepares us to release the cry that will melt the ice of the past. But being influential will be of no use if you trample and offend others. As you become more capable of gaining influence, you must work twice as hard to demonstrate that you have the dignity to bear it.

 ## GIVE IT YOUR ALL

Effective influence, like a radiant sword, is a blade we must know how to carry. We need to have it in a sheath of responsibility and decorum, of prudence and humility. We can summarize this as the grace of kindness. What a great and forgotten virtue! It's a rotting fruit among today's selfishness and lack of empathy. We walk so quickly that we unknowingly step on pieces of others beneath our feet.

But how beautiful and sublime is the kindness that human beings have as a result of their good essence. To meet a kind being is to meet someone who has a great appreciation for human dignity and everything around them, whether that be animals, plants, or things. The kind person has a special virtue: reconciling the universal individual. We are kind if we're friends, if we're genuine. A person who is kind to others treats them like family, which is actually linked to *kind*'s Old English root, *kin*, which means to belong to a family.

It's so difficult not to be carried away by anger, annoyance, physical pain, rage, apathy, or bad gestures and rudeness toward others. Therefore, kindness training should be a top concern in society, at home, and at work. Kindness helps us escape the law of the jungle. Kindness is one of the most important traits of a noble heart. Being kind is also a talent that costs zero cents but adds a significant value to everyone in the community. How hard is a human relationship when you have to tolerate or cope with a rude or temperamental person! Those people with moody expressions and gloomy energy don't smile, they just grimace. They obscure everything around them. Some people think the word *kindness* is easy to say, but we often struggle to do so due to weariness, indifference, and modern tiredness that leave no room for the most beautiful part of humanity. Our days pass in silence and in the coldness of stern expressions next to the people we love the most.

We are chilled by other people's lack of kindness, and because of them we distrust humanity. In its absence, we forget to embrace our souls and our hearts wither. We cease to kindle love in others when we turn our backs on kindness. To be kind is to learn to live between scarcity and excess, to turn opacity into brilliance, to be strong beyond muscles.

TO BE KIND IS TO
KINDLE LOVE IN OTHERS.

Be kind and become a torch that kindles love and tenderness in others. Be kind and disarm the hearts of others. Be kind and bring peace to whatever you do and wherever you are.

But be careful, because by confusing kindness with commitment, hundreds of times we've said to ourselves, "I gave it my all." Generally speaking, that's great, yet there are situations where, although it may sound romantic, poetic, and even caring, the tyrannical demands we're asking of ourselves are absolutely exhausting. We even give what we don't have, like a gambler who expects to win double or nothing when they gamble away their last assets.

Some people go so far as to give their all as a manipulative mechanism. They're the same ones who keep quiet to avoid conflict but then experience the conflict of not speaking up. There are those who claim to live without attachments but complain that no one pays for their expenses. The environment ends up taking advantage of those who absurdly long for the happiness of others and forget their own. They save a person and then they have to save themselves from that person. In their intimate world they haven't discovered why it's difficult for them to be happy. For them, every pleasure is a source of guilt. Delight distresses and shames them. They don't allow themselves to be happy because they believe pain is the right way to express themselves. They know no other story than that of suffering for others.

Although empathy is born when the pain of others is in your heart, it will only be valuable if your heart is full of love. When people give too much, they don't dare to enjoy life except through someone else. They say they love others, but that's meaningless if they don't love themselves. Human love is not inexhaustible like a love feast, like the love of God, the source of which is endless.

These people give their time, effort, and money, and say it's free, but their emotional imbalance goes bankrupt. They don't protect themselves. They never take time for themselves. They give expecting to receive, and that makes them slaves of a void. They owe themselves massive quotas of love, and accumulate thousands of disappointments, because the world doesn't love the way they understand love.

If what you've read in the last few paragraphs resonates with you, check your heart. I don't want you to continue to be disappointed by the world because you aren't receiving as much as you're giving. To give yourself time is to give yourself happiness. No one will come save you from your own void—it's up to you whether you give of yourself only to break down or you do it to gain momentum. You can run to flee or to really take off.

IT'S NOT ABOUT THE HEAVY SIGH,

IT'S ABOUT WHO CAUSES IT.

REVENGE DESTROYS, BUT
FORGIVENESS
IS DEVASTATING.

If you want to roar, you must firmly hold your breath before letting it out—it could come out as a sigh or as a bellow; that's up to you. Similarly, pain can be like a storm that lifts you up and allows you to take flight or leaves you sinking in the mire.

Without pain, life loses much of its meaning. Death is the force that enlivens and unveils the purpose of our journey.

 ## THE BRAVE ————————————————

Ever since I was a child, I have been exposed and willing to work under extreme circumstances. I have learned to persevere between beasts and spears. I was raised by absences and solemnities. That's why my hand doesn't tremble when I have to take risks, because I've lost everything and yet God has given me the strength to bring about great results under the worst conditions.

Life taught me not to wait for the perfect circumstances, but to make them happen. The rocky ground forged me and helped me build a reputation for accomplishing seemingly impossible missions and terrifying dreams. I'm one of the people who make a difference between defeat and victory. I have the incalculable good fortune of having a beautiful team that has allowed me to reach peaks. Without them I wouldn't have gotten there, and would have yearned for them.

I thank you for supporting the deeply flawed guy that I am, who also deeply loves to serve you with his soul. Just as you may now be redrawing the map of your life, many years ago I decided to live to train daily while others only longed for their dreams. I lined up in the ranks of that eternal army, and there, under the mantle of the Celestial General, I learned to endure doubts, uncertainties, judgments, and betrayals. I learned to walk in the crossfire, even though my legs were shaking. I am constantly tweaking my mind to be willing to tolerate high temperatures and pressures, and in doing so, I'm tearing down the enemy's strongholds, the walls of oppression. And now, finally, the chains are no longer holding my life back.

I know the harsh discipline of the caves, and I've never gotten used to comfort and ease. Why? Every day brings us closer to death. But wait, I don't find this discouraging, for I await it carrying the rod of eternity that gives me breath in the face of any valley of shadow or death.

I've learned to live intensely because I'm aware of the possibility that tomorrow I may not see the sunset again, so I act with energy, with passion, I am full of vigor and my dreams are the size of God. In Christ I have learned not to negotiate with doubt, and in Him I am capable of this and more. In Him I am an all-terrain, I like the roads less traveled and off the beaten track. I'm full of mistakes and anxieties, but I escape the feeling of suffocation because I don't see pain as a problem but as an opportunity to ride wildly. I take anguish and put a boot on pain's neck.

I AM ONE WHO FIGHTS
BATTLES FOR OTHERS
**JUST TO SEE THEM
SMILE AGAIN.**

I CHOOSE
TO LOVE

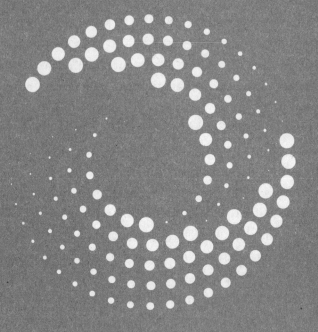

with all its consequences.

After the self-awareness processes and fine-tuning of your work plans, which we've reviewed in the first two steps of this book, it's time to be brave, to fulfill life's commitments with stewardship, and to learn to roar, because those who roar don't justify themselves, they overcome tiredness, laziness, and idleness, and they never make excuses. They are diligent to the grave.

Those who roar know that their destiny is a decision. They don't leave it to mystery and much less to the moods of the day. They move forward because they're bold, seizing opportunity after opportunity, no matter what it looks like. The brave recognize other brave people and join them—together they conquer dreams. The brave are easily recognized by their stained, torn leather suit and toothless mouths, but they smile from the joy of doing the impossible. There are no brave people in spotless suits.

To roar is not a slogan, much less a simple word. To roar is a daily and higher goal, it's a way of life, it's a divine vision.

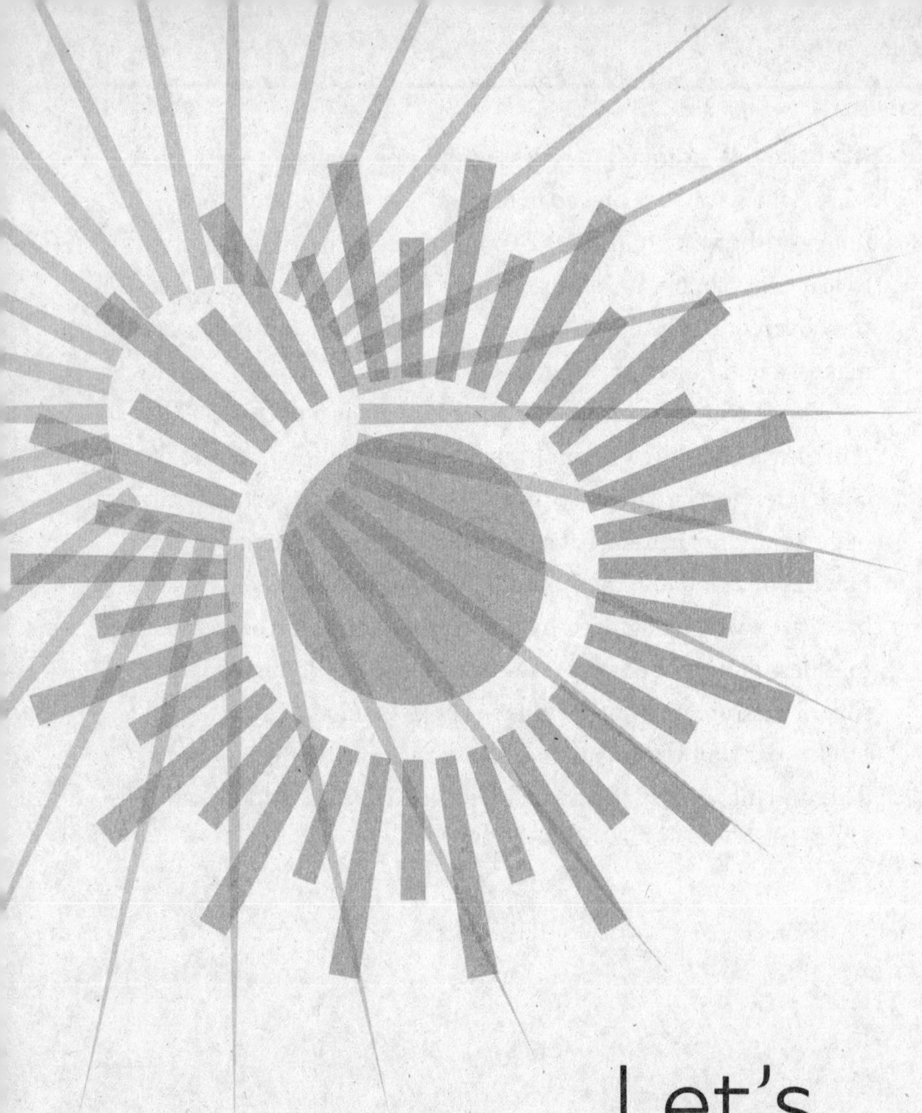

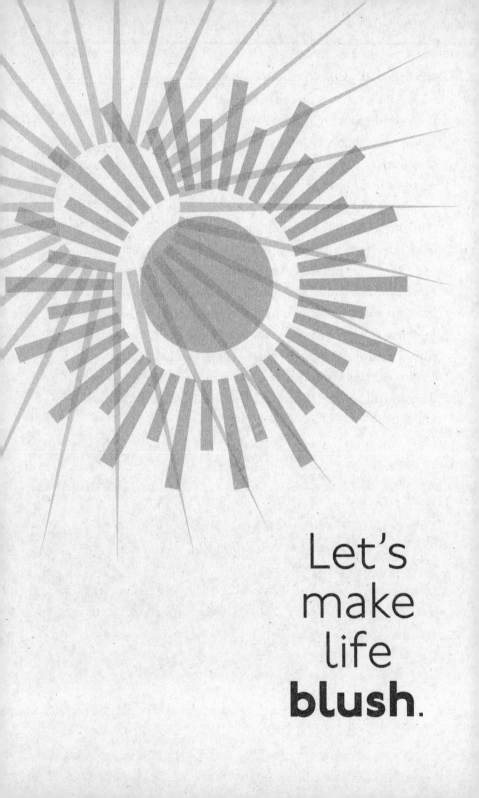

ROAR

One day, you just stop waiting and wake up with the attitude of someone who's sure that they've been holding back what they want to shout for too long. Your chest, swollen with effort and passion, is stronger than steel armor and contains the powerful energy of eternity's artilleries. The breaths of fire are your desire for victory. The unruly flames are your longing to crush the doubts that were deposited on you, the reproaches and ridicule that you received when you insisted on preparing to unleash the irrepressible power that you carry within you.

Now is the time for you to buckle down and keep your willpower stronger than ever, resist with persistence, and understand that self-control will allow you to seal the leak through which the pressure you have concentrated can seep. It will serve as a saber to defend you from the temptations of immediate joys and the siren song of weaknesses. You owe it not only to who you are now, but who you will be after you've deployed the shrapnel of your talent.

With all the pieces you've gathered about you, and the mastery you've acquired to arrange them strategically, you'll be able to combine your desires with your skills, your profitability with your contributions. This doesn't take away from the fact that your development naturally brings growth in your personal well-being, resources, freedom, joy, and productivity. This map re-creates the battlefield you must invade.

LOVING. I DON'T KNOW ANY OTHER WAY TO LIVE.

Once you decide to command the front line of your cry, you'll be unstoppable on your way to total victory. But this will not come without changes. You will leave behind the people who have anchored you to the past, you will rebuild what you understand to be mistakes, and you will even have a new perspective about the final day.

Yes, it will hurt to tread on the parched field of betrayals and lies. Yes, there will be distortions that will attempt to extinguish what is rumbling within you. Yes, the battle will also include setbacks and defeats. Even so, this is the defining phase, the one that will prevent you from being devoured by your fears and doubts, the false limitations you've imposed on yourself, and the deaf noise of criticism that doesn't let you hear that your opportunity has arrived.

Roar, because you have no choice but to choose between thunder and silence.

 ## SELF-CONTROL

Releasing the roar goes beyond a moment of enthusiasm; it requires a series of efforts. Today's cry is only possible because it's composed of many heartbeats that were held back when we wanted to let go, to stop resisting, to take a sweet breath, even if in that sigh we lost the whirlwind's intensity.

When you decide to move from the inflame phase to the roar phase, you're giving up everything that has been holding you back. To avoid returning to that spot, you need an essential ingredient: self-control. This is the power we use to manage our desires, emotions, and behaviors when we need to lean toward what we consider right, which also helps us achieve our goals.

A good example of self-control is choosing an hour of intense training at the gym over lying in bed with your phone as your scenery, water over soda, studying over partying. The key in this process is that we are exchanging one gain for another: an immediate and tangible pleasure for a distant and undefined one. We avoid eating a delicious chocolate bar because we have a clear motive: to improve our health, weight, or figure. But this benefit will not happen in the short term. What's more, our final goal doesn't just depend on this small sacrifice but on a series of them. Yet the joy we derive from eating that chocolate can be fully encompassed in quantity and time. We're rejecting a clear and certain satisfaction for a greater yet uncertain one. There's no greater pleasure than beating ourselves. You'll never regret yesterday's discipline and your future self will always be proud of you.

No different are the temptations that come from certain emotions, impulses, or desires, which we must control to achieve prosperity and quality of life.

Self-control is not a new concept; the Word already advised us, "He that is slow to anger is better than the mighty; and he that ruleth his spirit than he that taketh a city" (Proverbs 16:32). It is mentioned once and then gently emphasized by the insistence that self-control is greater than the treasures of all the plunder of kings and their armies. Fortunes are more than expendable resources; with self-control, we can always generate more.

MY CHALLENGE IS TO CONTINUE
TO ASK GOD FEWER QUESTIONS
AND LISTEN TO HIM MORE.

To those who believe that biblical texts aren't enough to explain human phenomena, let me tell you about a transcendent scientific study whose results coincide with the wisdom contained in Scripture. Aside from its revealing content, this research is enriched by the ingenuity and innocence that only children can bring. The experiment was conducted with students at the Bing Nursery preschool near Stanford University, where the daughters of the project's director, psychology professor Walter Mischel, were studying.

Mischel came from a Jewish family that had left their country, Austria, when it fell under the rule of Nazi Germany. Settling in Brooklyn, like thousands of other displaced persons, had a transformative impact on that child and left the grown man and researcher with a burning desire to explore the factors that determine perseverance and improvement. Understanding the configuration of self-control was an enigma that Mischel had long wanted to solve, and he found the answer in the ingenuousness of the children at Bing Nursery.

The study that his team developed in that preschool is, in my opinion, one of the finest and most fruitful findings in the history of the study of human behavior. It didn't just illustrate clues as to why successes and failures occur, but it also made it possible to monitor the effects that self-control has on more intimate dimensions of life.

The group of researchers began a series of tests to find out how children coped with the need to choose between an immediate and a future benefit. The test was carried out with students who were older than three years (old enough to understand the instructions), but younger than six (innocent enough in the calculation of their reactions). The lure needed to be something that the kids would see as valuable while also allowing them to reflect on the instructions, so the researchers decided to ask them to choose between eating one candy or eating two.

Before we proceed, I'd like to note that scientific studies like this one are often much more sophisticated than how we usually present them. To be brief and didactic, I've simplified some of the procedures without altering the results or conclusions, which are accurately expressed in this chapter. That specific study is even more complex because it spanned several decades. Since I know you'll find this subject fascinating, I invite you to read Mischel's own account in the book where he summarizes the findings of his five-decade-long research: *The Marshmallow Test: Understanding Self-Control and How to Master It.*[1]

Rather than a scientific procedure, this study is reminiscent of a joke from a hidden camera program. The researchers took the children to an area of the school that they called the "Surprise Room." After gaining the children's trust, the collaborator suggested a challenge: She told them that she would leave a candy on the table and exit the room for a while; if upon returning, the evaluated students had not eaten the candy, she would give them an additional one.

SUPPORT IS A BEAUTIFUL
AND ENDANGERED WORD.

The challenge was clear: eat one immediately with certainty or make a sacrifice and wait for the promise of receiving two. In the language we'll be exploring, we can look at it this way:

Instant gratification: This is the candy the researcher leaves in the room. We can enjoy it right now, without making an effort to wait for it, just as we enjoy many pleasures, even if they're counterproductive to our desires.

Delayed gratification: This is the pleasure of eating twice as many treats, as a result of the effort involved in waiting for a higher reward. It causes a momentary discomfort, but we're confident that it will be worth it because that effort leads us to a higher pleasure, like getting good grades after giving up several outings with friends during finals.

From the outset, the results were revealing. The first thing the researchers found was the series of resources the children, even the youngest ones, used to convince themselves to wait. They generally understood that it was worthwhile to hold out, even if they didn't do so. Naturally, we understand that sacrifices will have a favorable conclusion in the long run. We don't need to reach adulthood to understand that waking up early to study is a better choice in the long run than staying in bed. This is something we know whether we get out of bed or not. This inner conviction leads us to develop methods that help us curb the desire to take the bait of immediate pleasure.

What the children did while they waited in the Surprise Room reveals how difficult it was to pass this test. Some would move away from the temptation with strategies such as turning their backs to the treat or covering their eyes. Others would approach it and caress it or rub it on their faces without actually taking a bite.

Oftentimes marshmallows were used to tempt the children. That's why this study is popularly known as the Marshmallow Test. You can use this name to find more information about it in books, videos, and references. If you want to have fun, search the internet for videos related to the "Marshmallow Test"; this will help you better understand the experiment and you will see the enormous efforts made by the children subjected to this test to achieve the greatest possible benefits.

THE POWER OF WAITING

After the publication of the first results, the subject was forgotten in scientific circles, but as time went by, Mischel wanted to know what had become of the thirty or so children who had participated in the project. He went back to the school with a set of questions, and the answers were shocking. The same children who had displayed the greatest willpower to get the second marshmallow after a few years showed superior performance in most of the basic educational and social indicators. This difference wasn't because they were smarter or came from more educated or wealthier homes. The only common factor among this group of children was their ability to self-regulate, which was an essential fuel for achieving their goals.

I GOT THE BILL I OWED FOR
SEVERAL STUPID THINGS THIS MONTH.

The development of self-control is triggered by personal drive. Those who show the ability to resist giving up an immediate plea-

BEHOLD

YOURSELF IN

THE MIRROR

AND DON'T

LOOK AWAY

FROM THE

REFLECTION

sure with the intention of obtaining a greater one are much more likely to achieve success in different dimensions.

Imagine that you've set a series of goals that you can only achieve by giving up things that provide you with enormous satisfaction. If your desire is to excel in music, you'll have to put in many hours of practice today to reach the level of proficiency that can only be achieved over the years. The same goes for sports, business, and many other dreams you may want to pursue. None of them will be possible if you don't put tomorrow's success before today's party.

The study didn't end with the children's academic performance. After these clues, Mischel kept following for decades the students to whom he offered marshmallows in the late 1960s, recording the aspects that he considered most susceptible to being affected by strong or weak self-regulation: health, stability, and personal relationships. When those same Bing Nursery children were nearing thirty years of age, they continued to show personal and professional performances that reflected their self-control: Those who couldn't wait for the treat as preschoolers and succumbed to instant gratification had a higher body mass index than those who could wait for a future reward.

This attribute has greater implications than showing strength when tempted by an appetizing sweet. It has nothing to do with the relationship between treats and physical appearance. Its explanation lies in the mental plane: Those who as children could not bear to wait for a reward and chose to eat the treat on average showed a lower perception of themselves, a less efficient handling of stressful situations, and a higher rate of addiction to different substances and drugs. As if this weren't enough, they also had lower levels of education and higher divorce rates.

On the other hand, the children who had shown signs of self-control rated better decades later in all the aforementioned indicators and also had greater resources to deal with adverse social situations.

Check out this example. I make you an offer: $5 million right now or one penny doubled the first month, and the new amount doubled the following month, and so forth. Which would you choose? Answer honestly.

If you choose the second option, at the end of the first month you'd only have two measly pennies, instead of immediately having $5 million. After a year, you'd look back at your little penny and see that it had amounted to around twenty dollars. You'd sigh and regret your "stupid" decision. You'd leave the money there and try to forget that mistake.

HOW DANGEROUS
ARE THOSE WHO THINK THEY DON'T NEED ANYONE!

Two more years go by and you're surprised by a call from the bank. The manager is requesting a meeting with you. You remember your penny, and when you check your account, you see that your balance has exceeded $343 million. You were right to bet on the future.

That's what it's like to bet on the future. In the moment, we think that a penny isn't going to make a difference. If you train for an hour today, you'll weigh the same tomorrow, you won't notice any changes, but that doesn't mean it's ineffective. It's a gamble that multiplies itself like your shy penny.

Invest in yourself. Your willingness yields the highest growth rate. You are the best long-term investment and a business that runs no other risk than trying. Stand firm during downturns because it's precisely in crises that stocks offer us their highest returns. You count on divine support, so you will never be without means if you lean on faith.

Multiply yourself with a future bet, with the absolute confidence that the investment you make in yourself will need to draw new graphs to hold you. You are the currency that doubles in value with each wager. You are the swollen ground of riches you are now building. Persevere and don't depreciate yourself. If you stand firm, you will trade up.

Your tenacity surpasses the value of metals and precious stones. Your discipline redefines the mathematics of indices. Your heart of gold protects you. No liquidity is more valuable than the sweat of your efforts. No closing is more valuable than the times you've said no because you believe in a higher yes.

I'll put my money on you. Your value will double every day.

 ## OUR MARSHMALLOWS

Going back to the penny exercise, you could tell me that you don't know if you'll still be alive in three years, so you'd prefer the five million from the start. But that would show you lack faith and purpose and have no goals worth reaching or living for. If you prefer the five million because you don't know what the future has in store for you, then you should eat without moderation, get into unlimited debt, and cancel your insurance. Would you do that? Of course not. Then you do believe in the future.

Let's look at the marshmallow choices of our life: an affair or marital strength, laziness or a professional career, comfort or a transformative project. Each of these elements is linked to knowing that our future achievements require a disciplined today. We will always be faced with the choice of either giving pleasure to who we are now or making the effort to please that hazy being we will be in a few years.

THERE'S A LOT OF POWER
IN THOSE WHO
KEEP THEIR PROMISES.

As we saw in the Marshmallow Test, the balance tips in favor of those who choose to postpone pleasure in order to make it grow. Standing firm in the face of temptation turned out to be a predictor of healthier personal behavior, less aggression, better grades—though that's not related to intelligence—a tendency toward stability in personal relationships, and better learning rates. The balance always moved in favor of those who had chosen to postpone pleasure to make it grow.

These children were unknowingly announcing what their tendency would be as adults. However, the fact that this is an innate condition doesn't justify what we do as adults. The time for considering yourself innocent for not being able to resist life's temptations at every moment is over. Just because your self-regulation has been weak up until now doesn't mean you're destined to fail. Self-control can be strengthened. Willpower is like a body that is toned with practice and knowledge. If you believe you would've been one of those children who did not resist temptation, you can change this reality, or continue to compete against adversaries who have a leg up on you. The most outstanding athletes are those who combine effort and knowledge, even when they're up against physically advanced opponents.

Since this is a struggle between current and future pleasure, one way to minimize that distance is to create certain immediate trade-offs. In other words, you should reward yourself when you invest in your future. Think of it as an advance on profits. Set up an account where you can deposit points every time you choose well. This is much more than a metaphor. You can set compensation criteria that you can turn into a concrete profit whenever you wish.

Let's say you take time to study Mandarin, training that may be a deciding factor in your promotion. You traded the pleasure of watching a popular series for time spent studying a language that will require several months to see slight progress. If you reach a benchmark, such as five hours, you can turn it into something that can be used as a reward. In a way, you will get a reward in advance, but it will become an investment you'll make in creating habits and rapid progress. Before long you'll see that there's no greater pleasure than making progress in what you want.

If you stay active, you'll have fewer chances of finding yourself in a situation where you could make the wrong choice. The popular saying is true: "I'm too busy on my own grass to notice if yours is greener," to which I'd add that you don't have time to notice how green your grass is either. Work, especially work that requires mental effort, places us in circumstances that reduce our willingness to engage in unnecessary conflict. At the end of the day, you should focus on how many times your partner smiles when you're with them, how your children are behaving, how much time you've spent cultivating yourself, and turn that into a reward you collect in the present.

AN OPEN AND WILLING HEART
IS A MUSEUM OF BLESSINGS.

There are tools to help us stay on track. Since it's often difficult to decide on rewards and willpower plays against us, we can "automate" our responses with the implementation intention method. This was developed in Germany by Peter Gollwitzer to help people put their intentions into practice and improve their habits in the long term. When I use the word *automate*, I mean predetermining a response to certain stimuli and creating a plan for when, where, and how you're going to act.

Here's how this implementation works. We set up an action that we find hard to activate on our own, and we do it without having to think about what we're doing. For example, we can say to ourselves, "After brushing my teeth in the morning, I'll go for a jog." "Each time I see the neighbors, I'll take my blood pressure." "When I enter the elevator, I'll check my bank account balance."

This works because often the mental processes we use to take action lead us into a maze of worry and we end up doing nothing. We don't always find the motivation, we convince ourselves that we don't have the bandwidth, or we rationalize that it's not the right time.

The idea is to connect a specific situation to an expected action defined by you. Although this suggestion may sound too basic, this technique has been proven to be effective in creating positive habits and has been favorably tested to create appropriate habits in children.

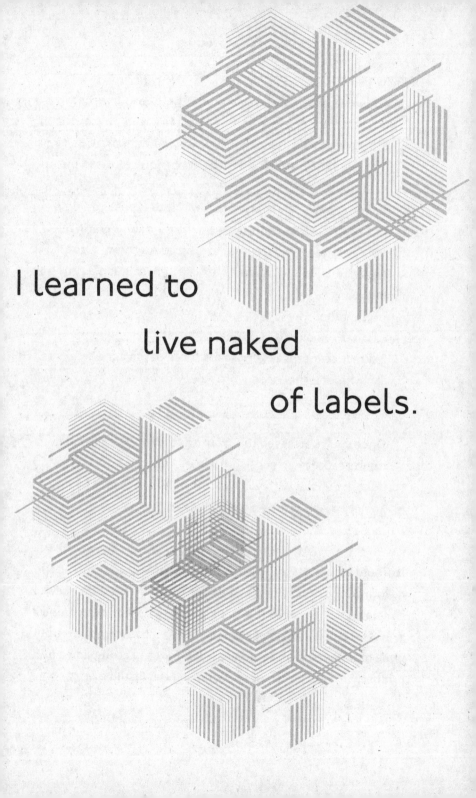

I learned to

live naked

of labels.

As we've seen, self-control can help you overcome any challenge and the more you hone it, the more effective you'll become. The way to achieve this is precisely by exercising actions that require you to put it to the test.

The simplest and most direct way is to expose yourself to situations that require you to forgo instant gratification, and see if you're able to overcome them. A good example is taking on complex challenges such as the following:

1. Go three days without eating sugar
2. Practice intense exercise for three days in one week
3. Write one thousand words a day for a week

Once you've achieved this, you can level up. For example, don't restrict just sugar for three days, but also flours. (Please consult with your doctor before engaging in any activity that involves dietary changes.)

It would be almost impossible to maintain a commitment and devote all the necessary effort to self-control if we didn't have a concrete goal. So far in this book, we've gone through complex processes of self-assessment and then perspective formulation, but none of this would make any sense if it weren't accompanied by a profound reason for taking the actions this demands.

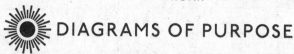

DIAGRAMS OF PURPOSE

There are too many obstacles and too long a road to reach our loftiest dreams. At the same time, this is a journey we take not just to reach the destination and stay there. Sometimes we must climb down from success to see it through.

THE SOUL'S MEMORY CAN
ALWAYS STORE ALL THE DATA.

How to identify the purpose that should move us is a topic that has been covered endlessly, and various theories have been developed, many of them effective. When considering which one to recommend, I prefer one that combines what we're passionate about (what we love) with what comes naturally (what you're good at, that is, what your intelligence supports), what is transcendent (what the world needs, meaning the contribution we make), and what is profitable (what we can be paid for, in other words, the compensation our actions yield).

The theory that I will explain in the following pages comes from the ingenuity of several thinkers whose ideas eventually found a common path, even though their disciplines weren't seeking the same outcome. Their combined work doesn't offer an easy-to-apply alternative for moving forward individually in terms of personal purpose. But it possesses a vision that has become an extraordinary phenomenon.

The first step was taken by astrologer Andrés Zuzunaga. Just to be clear, I don't subscribe to astrological concepts, but this model is very useful whether you do or not. Zuzunaga proposed a Venn diagram depicting the interrelation of the four factors I just mentioned above. The intention of this diagram was to illustrate his view of the forces at work in the construction of our purpose.

A couple of years later, author Marc Winn fused basic interpretations of certain branches of Japanese philosophy with the graphic representation designed by Zuzunaga. Winn presented his model to summarize the concept of *ikigai*—which refers to where the source of the value of life emerges and gives meaning to our effort—and ended up creating a new guide for evaluating our actions in the map of the aforementioned dimensions: what we're passionate about, what comes naturally, what is transcendent, and what is profitable.[2]

This new diagram has become so popular that in the Western world it has turned into an icon for understanding, exploring, and explaining the principles of *ikigai*, which hasn't been welcomed by some experts on the subject, but has become a didactically exceptional and popular tool.

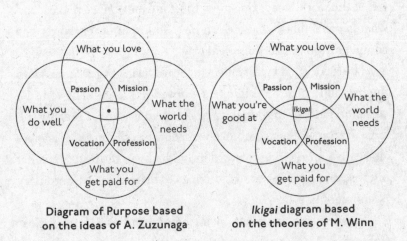

Diagram of Purpose based on the ideas of A. Zuzunaga

***Ikigai* diagram based on the theories of M. Winn**

After Winn adapted the diagram, it went viral, and this vision is now indivisible from *ikigai*, given that practically all the literature on the subject is based on this interpretation, although unfortunately an alarming number of authors have forgotten to mention its creators.

In the *ikigai* model proposed by Winn, which stems from his own interpretation of this Japanese philosophy, the tasks of daily survival converge with the highest elements of each person, through their skills, astuteness, and ingenuity. These are things that can make us happy and become our livelihood.

From a more philosophical perspective, this vision seeks to make people do things in a sustainable and harmonious way. Under *ikigai*, everyday activities are enjoyed and value is placed on small details.

IF THEY ARE NOT STIMULATED, THE HEARTBEATS LOSE THEIR RHYTHM.

Each of the circles in the diagram proposed by Winn represents one of the four factors that, when connected, lead to what he calls *ikigai*:

- What we love to do and we'd do without looking at the clock or how much we get paid for it.
- What supports our natural intelligences. We feel comfortable doing it because we do it well (and ideally, we love doing it).
- What we can do to receive an income. We've already established a way to turn it into a source of income. (And it would be even better if we were passionate about doing it and were good at it).

- An activity that gives back, fulfills us, and gives meaning to our lives. (It would be perfect if we were excited just thinking about it, exhibited mastery in its execution, and were compensated for doing it).

The interaction of these four factors, whether they're referred to as "*ikigai*" or "purpose," also has other internal connections that can be seen in the following illustrations.

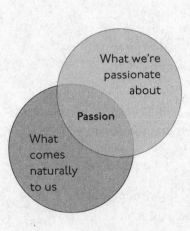

When what we are passionate about is combined with what comes naturally to us, we have a passion, an activity that we enjoy doing, and we do it well, like the skilled dancer who can spend all day on stage and who is scolded because they need to rest.

We mustn't forget that passion comes from *passio*, which means "to suffer" and is related to *padecer*, which also means "to suffer," as in the Passion of Christ, who received the action. In our passion, we are the subject.

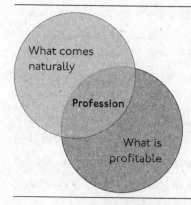

When what is supported by our natural intelligences is combined with what we can do to support ourselves financially, we have a profession, the job we're paid to do well.

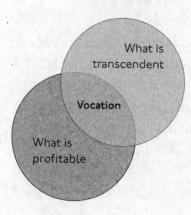

When what we are paid to do is combined with the transcendent, we find a vocation. For example, the social work we do and for which we receive financial compensation. The vocation must come from our ideals and convictions, not from what benefits us.

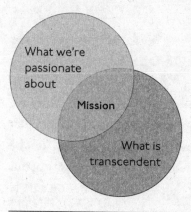

When the transcendent is combined with what we're passionate about, we have a mission, which can be a kind of personal priesthood, something that is done mainly because it generates enthusiasm in ourselves and others. This can be common in volunteer or activist activities.

While connecting the factors in the previously mentioned combinations can be beneficial, none of them can provide you with a lasting purpose on their own. If any of these connections aren't made, a vacuum is created that will eventually swallow that purpose because it is incomplete.

In my case, I'd add to the four dimensions my constant search for ways to place my steps on the mantle of God's will. God is in what I'm passionate about, and my talents are a gift He has bestowed me. Similarly, any resource received comes from His grace, and any transcendent action is a compensation for His favors.

For example, we could do something that we like, that fulfills us, and that we do well, but it would be difficult to make it sustainable if it doesn't offer us financial support. Similarly, if a job that we're good at is financially profitable, but doesn't end up moving us, sooner or later we'll be filled with dissatisfaction and we'll seek to intensify one of the other factors (more money or greater social contribution, for example). In other words, if you're good at a job and it's profitable financially, but you're not passionate about it, sooner or later you may feel that you need more money to make up for that.

DON'T WORRY WHEN I RUN OUT OF PATIENCE, BUT RATHER OF DESIRE.

If we embark on activities that do nothing for the community, we will lose our chance to leave a legacy. If we engage in activities that don't match our talents, we'll be overworked and that will likely be a source of distress and fatigue. As you can see, the intensity of our purpose can be drained by any of those four leaks, but on a daily basis, in the demanding world we live in, the one that consumes the most time and has caused us the most sleepless nights is the one that has to do with money. You need to take some diligent time to locate yourself on the map of life and know where you stand and where the heck you're going. Shake off your apathy right now, dot your *i*'s and cross your *t*'s.

INTENTION MAP

The fear of going bankrupt or of losing the income we rely on, even if it's coming from an activity that destroys us from within, is the main reason why millions of people in the world are afraid to release the butterflies and pursue their personal purpose. Since this is precisely the most critical element in the modern era, I will devote the next two sections of this step to talking a bit about money, but first let's finish our review of the purpose model.

Let's take a look at what we've just discussed with a concrete example: music, an activity that many people are passionate about. To turn music into a purpose, aside from passion, one must have musical intelligence (this activity's contribution to society is so important that we don't even need to mention it). You may already have these three factors in place, but turning a musical career into a way of life becomes a bit more complicated. It's not always about whether we have the courage to let our dreams take flight, but whether we are willing to give them wings.

Before we continue, remember that achieving your purpose doesn't imply that you should abandon other vital issues for you and your loved ones. On the contrary, it should become the engine that drives your relationships with greater intensity. This exercise

IT'S FORBIDDEN

TO STOP DREAMING.

doesn't consist of finding a purpose and only focusing on it—you must remain in a constant state of seeking.

With an idea that you consider one of your dreams, use the purpose model to answer the four essential questions that will help you see if that activity could become a life purpose:

- Am I really passionate about it and do I love it?
- Do I have the natural ability to do it?
- Is it transcendent for society?
- Can I turn it into a monetizable activity?

While this is not enough to determine a life purpose, it's a starting point that will give you clarity and help you build a much clearer path toward your dreams.

Although the letter on which you will write your destiny is a blank sheet of paper today, you won't find what you're looking for on a piece of paper or in a diagram method. That will only hold the beginning of a plan, a proposal. This has an obvious philosophical aspect, but it also has a practical one that we must pay attention to. At the same time, never forget that flexibility is essential, always being ready to take unexplored paths. The boxer's waist is what allows them to dodge blows in each new round. We must keep moving, making use of all the space, because the only way to get off of the ropes is to step up to the center of ourselves.

IT'S SO BEAUTIFUL WHEN
THE SPARK MEETS THE BREEZE.

Let's turn now to the most concrete aspect of this whole process: money. When the creators of the model incorporated the dimension "what I get paid," they didn't establish an amount, but we should think about it. "What I get paid" can be an empty criterion if we don't define it appropriately. The activities we seek to develop, the ones we'd like to devote ourselves to completely, should pay us at least for what we produce today.

I only want to show you that that this exercise begins with an intention map, which you'll use to define the necessary steps to build the life you desire. No one can give you a map with a clear and smooth road ahead of time. Looking at your purpose is the starting point, the blueprint that you must study before taking to the field. Then comes the hard part: making it a reality. Staying on the sidelines and imagining what it would be like to reach the land of your dreams is useless.

Moving beyond it depends on your attitude and determination to cause and create productive days. Once you feel you've accumulated enough preparation to charge forward, let go of your fears and doubts, sharpen your sword, and go forth wearing the armor of eternity. Forge ahead with the attitude and desire to grow beyond your expectations. Dare to outdo your own competition. The soul and spirit don't recognize fear because anxiety and panic are nowhere near this state. I know you will face circumstances that will raise walls in front of your goals, but believe me, you've worked hard to gain the strength to tear them down.

Self-control from the spirit is the most effective form of physical and mental control. Making decisions and navigating the twists and turns of uncertainty and of life's anxieties are signs of maturity and gratitude. No fear will be irrevocable, so hold the urge in your chest and let your cry carry action and execution. Only then will you receive the echoes of triumph.

The key is to find the action that satisfies all aspects: Start with passion; you'll build the rest from there. I love writing; that's why I made writing a way of life. Then it became a profession. The commitment and love for my passion came long before the publishing contracts. If I had stopped writing because it didn't pay the bills, I never would've become someone who pays some bills with what he writes.

I put my purpose's vision into practice with my occupation as a writer. I sketched out my intention map and slowly but surely gained ground in faraway lands. The love of ink never ends. This love of ink allows me to write on paper or stone. Love is what finds a blank page where others left scratches. Love is what led me to do the small things with excellence and then reach the pinnacle of my skills.

Much of my fulfillment comes from writing. I'm someone who wants to give away words until the fingers of my soul and my hands are splintered from the need to express themselves. That's my erogenous zone: I want to finish with all the blank pages.

I WRITE AND GOD TAKES CARE OF ERASING, CROSSING OUT, CORRECTING, COLORING, AND ADDING THE LAST PERIOD. **I AM THE PEN; HE IS THE INK.**

The author can die of love or sadness while writing their process. The writer grows with each betrayal, so I stitch my wounds with ink and paper. I want to write until I strip myself of all ties. I will not out of cowardice or negligence allow someone else to write my story. I want to spend entire nights in a metaphor, or let a quill ask my heart to dance.

I am made of marble, of foam, of tears. I can be whoever I am. I believe those who love life grab their pen and write their future. My vice is writing. I like art, the sonnet, and baroque concepts, lyricism, versification, celestial allusions—even a hyperbaton moves me. I write to breathe, to experience what I cannot yet reach, but with letters I can touch.

If I write "Japan," I appear there. If I write "Heaven," angels rain down from the sky. For me, to write is to possess, to burn, to be ashes, a ghost, and to turn into a vigil. My pen is a steed that carries no saddle and, therefore, its freedom is wild and pure.

It fascinates me and adds to my fulfillment. It has become one of my sources of income, and with my words I send messages that I consider valuable to those who read me. I have a purpose, and I will continue to write.

What about you? What are you waiting for? Jump at the chance to make a living enjoying what you love and are most passionate about.

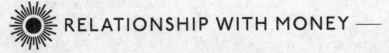 ## RELATIONSHIP WITH MONEY ⸺

I usually don't talk about this topic simply because it's not one of my priorities. As we have seen when we talked about purpose, money is no more than a result of my passions. But I do know that resources will keep coming to mind as you approach the edge of the summit, where you will be left with only two options: Turn back or take flight.

Over the years and with experience, I've come to realize that the relationship with money is one of the main barriers people face in reaching the depths of their dreams. And in many cases, it's related to the beliefs that we've formed about the importance of money in our lives.

To sum this up, there are two philosophical extremes, two sharp and opposite points that prevent us from imagining that following our desires is a way to generate income. On the one hand, there are those who refuse to turn what they love into a source of income, and on the other, those who refuse to try because they can't afford to stop producing income.

Thousands think that wealth is bad, and even hate it and those who have it. Let me show you what you despise: the ideological representation of the wealthy and all that goes with it.

While I agree that the idea of portraying that person as a scoundrel is appealing to most, this characterization is often misguided—in fact, it can be vague and basic. The world has stigmatized a role mostly constructed by the opinions of those who never managed to become wealthy.

I DON'T CHASE MONEY BECAUSE IT SEEMS TOO SLOW FOR MY SPEED.

This perspective is rooted in the culture of Latin American countries. This doesn't mean we're like this—there are notable examples to the contrary—but it is a common social tendency among us when comparing ourselves to people from other cultures.

We plunge into adulthood soaked in a downpour of technical and theoretical confusions that complicate our approach to wealth. We have a lousy relationship with our personal finances due to the fact that educational systems allocate marginal, almost nonexistent resources to subjects that have to do with the possession, management, and multiplication of resources. Even at universities, there's a fairly widespread view of money as something associated with vices and represented by wealthy people with strong negative values. From popular sayings to daily soap operas, there is an insistence on portraying the rich as reprehensible figures. Although we live in a society full of corruption, abuse, authoritarianism, and inequality, cases in which the possession of resources is due to one of these reasons alone will always be the exception.

Although it is very pronounced among our peoples, this perspective is not exclusive to Latin America. The Anglo-Saxon world repeats these patterns. From the earliest literature to TV series, and from children's stories to comic books, the great villains are rich, lonely, selfish, and bitter people. We could fill the book with characters who fit these attributes. From Lex Luthor to Cruella de Vil, there are many villains who share, among their main traits, the practically unlimited possession of resources.

We need to examine this mindset to see what makes it so strong, what its essential concepts and beliefs are, and why it's so prevalent among us. To begin with, this notion helps us justify what we have not achieved. What's more, if we insist on associating poverty with virtue, we will have gone a step further: "poor, but honest," as if honesty could kneel before a comma, as if we could not be "prosperous and honest." We've been taught to value poverty more than humility, vivaciousness more than ingenuity. Our leaders insist that being rich is bad, but it was never bad for them. We see the abundance but not the effort. We've been told it's good to save, but we've never been invited to invest. Politicians have said that salaries paid by companies are bad, but they put up a thousand obstacles for us to become entrepreneurs.

Life won't care about your reasons, but about your facts. Using false modesty hidden behind a double standard as an excuse is unacceptable. Let's say you have a million dollars in your head, but you don't know how to transfer it to your pocket. The formulas have changed and will continue to change, but it's time to stop hiding behind your circumstances.

MY DOUBTS FIT
IN MY TORN POCKET.

Money is one of the fruits of our labor. Whether it's bad or good depends on how you obtain it, but above all, on how you use it. It should always be a means, never an end. That's why convictions should never be for sale. I think it is likely that many of those who "hate money" probably hide behind that hatred the frustration of not knowing how to produce income in such a competitive, mutant, and voracious world. Those who criticize the sins of abundance are the first ones who would enter hell to enjoy them.

Just as there are those who despise money as a toxic entity, there are those who consider it a virtue in itself. This is another negative extreme, which ends up putting money above people. It's as harmful as the previous one when it comes to being productive. This is important because these ideas lead us to honestly believe that wealth is the consequence of a superior, almost ontological quality, and not the result of creativity, initiative, and a lot of effort, regardless of the fact that some start in the basement and others on the rooftop. The problem is that when a low-income person believes in this prejudiced view of society, they surrender to the belief that there are no alternatives. But being poor is a design, not a condition. These classist concepts try to instill in our minds that there's a predestination, that

THOSE
WHO
NEVER
BURN

CALL ME
"INTENSE."

effort is not enough to get ahead. And when push comes to shove, this almost celestial vision of wealth ends up being just as damaging as associating money with exploitation and deception.

 ## MAKING MONEY IS AN ART FORM

I believe that the right mindset is essential for a person to prosper financially. Again, it's impossible to get out of poverty without models that reconcile us with money. That's why it would be of great help to have an educational system that reconciled money with willpower and constant dedication.

I say this knowing that we live on a continent marked by profound inequalities. Coming from the most privileged segments of society offers advantages in loan acquisitions, educational systems, and family independence. Nevertheless, for all social sectors, having an efficient, accessible, and adequate education is essential for future challenges, allowing us to pave the way for those who follow us. In this case we come back to the issue of what we learn and practice. For example, it's very common to hear that Latinos have lower savings rates than other regions, but we don't know how to properly define savings. We continue to believe that it means having our assets in a bank or under a mattress.

I'VE NEVER SEEN ANYONE MAKE A LOT BY RISKING LITTLE

Most countries in North America and Latin America have experienced hyperinflation, and savings have lost their conventional meaning, yet we still haven't been able to redefine that term. In *The Psychology of Money* (2020), Morgan Housel describes some of the keys that shape our understanding of money. One is that our experiences shape our particular perspectives on how finance works.

The same author argues that even education can't help us fully re-create the experiences of other societies—maybe that's why we're so willing to make the same mistakes—yet, undoubtedly, as we become aware of the existence of resources, we increase our capacity to act. Unfortunately, our high school graduates leave school without even having heard the words *investment*, *dividend*, and *profitability*.

All these elements end up digging a ditch that makes it more complicated to reconcile ourselves with the images of prosperity. And when you roar, and your efforts begin to bear fruit, there will also be those who criticize you for what you have. The bloodthirsty attacks of those who do not accept your progress will come from every direction. I stopped paying attention to them when I realized how interested they were in how much I have and how little they cared about how hard I had worked to get it. I've been working for thirty years, twenty years of that before social media exploded onto the scene.

Let's get one thing straight: *working* is one thing, but there is a world of difference between that and *knowing how to work*. Making money is an art form, because it requires the use of creativity in an effective and productive way, being orderly and disciplined, being punctual and forever passionate, building a life in which work and family merge and coexist in synergy, knowing how to communicate and express oneself, knowing how to spend and invest, knowing how to hire and lead. To produce something, all of these art forms must merge and become one line.

Working shouldn't be a merit but a joy. And making money

should be considered an art form when done ethically. Never be ashamed of having money. We've been raised to feel bad about our accomplishments, about the grace and blessing we have achieved by being diligent, skillful, and tenacious.

When you reach your peak, many will say that it was handed to you or that it was sheer luck, that you were born with a silver spoon in your mouth, that you had more opportunities than others, that you stole, or that you cheated. They'll make public claims because they don't know how hard you worked in private, how much you've given for everything you have. Many will play the victim and that's why they'll never be leaders, because a leader who acts like a victim can't lead themselves or anyone else. So while others cry and point fingers at you, keep on harvesting and shattering those wine presses. Being held accountable by God will be enough.

I LOOK MORE LIKE WHAT YOU DON'T SEE
THAN WHAT YOU IMAGINE.

Earn all the money you want honestly and enjoy it. Relish it in the fragility of life, but above all, share it with others. Be prudent, devoid of greed. Invest a little, save a little, but never save yourself from experiencing moments. Spend without wasting your life. Save what you have in your pocket, but not what is in your heart. Never spare kisses, hugs, or good deeds. Never spare words of love.

Our relationship with money is not restricted to the amounts we deposit or withdraw from the bank. Money is much more complex than an exchange rate. If we were guided solely by the monetary denomination of money, we'd lose the sense of its value. This was already explained by the Spanish poet Antonio Machado when he wrote: "Only a fool thinks price and value are the same."

The latter is crucial when we add up how much we invest in the different steps that lead us to our goals. In human thinking, it's natural to be dominated by numbers. We unconsciously open a mental account for each type of expense, and in that account, we accumulate what we've invested. I will explain this mental accounting with the help of one of the most interesting behavioral studies I have ever read.

To put it in context: Money is supposed to be a "universal" exchange mechanism, which is why we value two products of the same price equally. According to this principle, with fifty dollars I can buy an earring or a good imported steak; I can also use that money to go to a soccer game or to the opera. So we could be led to think that the currency's value is preserved if things cost the same. In other words, losing a twenty-dollar bill should hurt just as much as ruining a tie of the same price.

On the other hand, the brain keeps a different record from our accounting books. It defines in advance what the money has been spent on and adds up all the amounts we have allocated for that purpose.

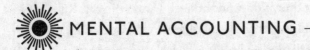 MENTAL ACCOUNTING

What we just discussed isn't only a theory. The marvelous duo of human research, the brilliant Daniel Kahneman and Amos Tversky, put this idea into practice by coming up with a brilliant experiment. They asked a group of students to imagine themselves in the following scenario: They had bought a ten-dollar ticket to a play. The researchers asked them to pretend that when they arrived at the theater door, they realized they had lost the ticket. The researchers then asked if they'd be willing to buy another ticket to see the play. Most participants said no.

The members of a second group were asked a different question: They were presented with the situation of going to a play where the ticket cost ten dollars, but in this case, they hadn't bought the ticket yet. But they had money in their pocket to do so. This group was asked to imagine that when they arrived at the box office, they noticed that they'd lost ten dollars of the total they had in their pocket, just like the previous group had lost the ticket. They were then asked the same question: Would they buy the ticket, even though they had lost the amount of money equal to the value of the ticket? The vast majority answered yes.

YOUR LIGHT IS IN YOU, NOT IN SOMEONE ELSE'S SHADOW.

In this hypothetical reality, the first group lost a ticket valued at ten dollars, and when they realized this, they chose to go home. The second group lost ten dollars that they had kept in their pocket, and still chose to see the play.

What explains these contradictory results? In the first case, they didn't enter the theater because their brain had already put ten dollars in the mental account for that event. In other words, they'd already paid for the play, and it would cost them twice as much if they bought another ticket. In the case of the second group, who lost plain old money, the brain lost the same amount in monetary terms, but the money hadn't been recorded in their mental accounts. So the play still cost ten dollars, but the lost money was not part of any personal calculation.

This illustrated how human beings mentally assign numerical criteria to certain activities.

Although, from a financial perspective, we should value two

products of the same price equally, our brains register them differently. We anticipate what we're going to spend the money on and establish a range of what we're willing to deposit into that account.

We can use this human thinking trait to our advantage and turn it into an opportunity to focus on future benefits. How? First, identify those future benefits you want to access, such as taking a trip with your family, taking a specific class, or buying something worth a lot of money. Once you determine the goal you're going to save for, you should begin to set aside a certain amount of money for this goal on a monthly basis. Many bank accounts today have a savings fund option where you can set aside money for a specific goal. For example, if you automate this and deposit twenty-five dollars into that fund each month, after four months you'll have saved one hundred dollars almost without even realizing it, because that amount is already mentally associated with a specific purpose.

Our brain registers and assigns different values in each case. This has great importance in how we make decisions, because by mentally allocating where resources go, we end up giving weight to what we contribute. The lost ticket was in an established mental account, the lost money was not related to any specific expense, but in theory both had the same value.

Why is this information important to roaring? Defining the right mental line items helps us create a more appropriate destination for our money. Additionally, if you manage to link it to your purpose, you'll have better results because you'll strengthen that connection. From a purely financial perspective, this approach has gained traction with the successful *Profit First* method popularized by entrepreneur Mike Michalowicz.[3] The idea behind that model is to allocate part of a business's return as profit and to separate other relevant expenses as structurally as possible.

I

BROUGHT

YOU

SOME

OF

WHAT

IS

LEFT

OF

ME.

Keeping this mental accounting can be very useful if we know what to do with it. Savings is a good example of this. In 2011, campaigns were launched to promote savings among workers in impoverished agricultural areas in Asia. At first, resources were focused on providing them with information that showed the benefits of financial planning, but there were no significant changes.

WHAT WE IGNORE IN OURSELVES
IS WHAT WE ATTACK WITHOUT MEASURE OR SCRUPLE IN OTHERS.

Despite the courses and offers that the workers received, the campaigns on the value of savings didn't cause any shifts in their financial habits. They received their salaries and spent them, leaving nothing for savings. This changed when it was suggested that workers receive their pay in two envelopes: one with the recommended savings percentage and the other with the rest of their salary. Nothing stopped them from spending the money; they were paper envelopes. The workers could easily open both envelopes and waste the money, but a significant group of them set that small amount aside for savings. What changed? This method activated the mental accounts that were intended for savings.

After this exercise, the savings promoters delivered the final punch: Inside the envelope with the savings, they inserted a photograph of the workers' children or other family members. This strategy reinforced the intention to save by directly linking the action with the benefit.

To apply this experiment to your life, the key is to develop the internal discipline to create the accounts that interest you: finish your graduate degree, publish your book, start that business. Before we move on, to be clear, when I talk about saving, I'm referring to a variety of options: We can save in currencies, investments, inventory, and other ways to protect and increase our money's value.

Regardless of your income level, set aside one or more accounts for your personal purposes. I'm not talking about mental records. I'm talking about creating real accounts that allow you to separate current expenses from your projects. Of course, in doing so, you'll limit your other resources. This will force you to take a closer look at your accounting and determine where you need to make adjustments.

Think of this exercise as the marshmallow of money: You can either choose to eat it now or make a sacrifice to invest those resources in what you so desire.

Now I'd like you to reflect on your personal stance regarding money. Do you feel you have a healthy relationship with money? Do you think you've prepared yourself to make money, beyond your professional training? What values do you communicate to your children about money? Do you think poverty is caused by external factors or is a result of individual decisions?

As we've seen, although we all want to improve our income, not all of us have an ideal relationship with money. That's why we must get used to doing the mental accounting that will allow us to have a better idea of what we have. We must also make an essential adjustment in our emotional accounts and how we relate to people. Just as we keep these records and organize our money, we also need to keep track of our affections and who occupies each place in the game.

Let go of the people who keep you tied to the past. Do it if you want to know what gifts the future holds for you. *Today's self* must know that *tomorrow's self* won't need them. These people can manipulate you and try to convince you that without them you won't get anywhere.

Blessed are the shores we reach after a shipwreck.

Let go of cowardice. You will walk in solitude, but each step will strengthen your abilities. God is with you; don't doubt it. The scales are tipped in your favor.

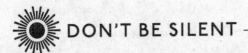 ## DON'T BE SILENT

We often think, *If I keep silent, if I keep quiet, if I take myself out of the equation, there is no conflict.* As if our silence could magically dismantle a problem. Sadly, this is often one of the methods used by people who say to themselves, "I don't like problems," and this is exactly how they approach and try to solve their issues, their stagnant liabilities.

I understand. I really do, because I have also tasted the bitter result that sometimes comes from saying what you feel. I have been involved in so many battles that sometimes I think I don't have the strength to face any more. That's why we must choose our battles wisely. We can't let fatigue be the reason our flanks are conquered. We must rise up. We can't defend our territory from within its walls. We must go outside.

Are you really going to let an invader of your happiness take what little freedom you have left? No, I'm not. Many believe the sensible thing to say is "The greatest victory is that which requires no battle," but most of the time this leads us to live in a false sense of peace, in a false sense of tranquility. You may be avoiding conflict with others, but you're failing to resolve the conflict within you.

Listen, every unfought war becomes an added defeat that we lose against ourselves. If you swallow what you feel, you accumulate pain. You will carry this burden and it will grow heavier by the day. It wouldn't make sense for me to ask you not to get angry. Of course you will. I'm asking you to not let anger stay inside you and corrode you.

Face yourself, you will win. Every time you advance, you will grow, you will learn. Don't stop, move forward, confront yourself. Remember that captains are only made in storms. Don't forget this lesson today, tomorrow, or ever.

Stop being silent, dare to speak. What you have to say matters. And express yourself face-to-face with everyone. Say what you must and watch them quickly start to leave, because most people love you just the way you are not.

Stop being silent, because not everything that makes noise breaks. Start making a little more noise, and God will join you in that battle where you must overcome yourself.

You also shouldn't remain silent when you've reached the point of exhaustion in any relationship. Speaking frankly is an act of responsibility. Dignity is fundamental to staying, but it's also fundamental when it's time to go. Leaving in silence, without expressing what we feel, is like leaving with someone else's heart and not paying the bill. When someone puts an end to the existing communication in a relationship with the intention of ending it suddenly, deliberately, and without explanation it's called *ghosting*. The person simply disappears: They become a ghost.

•

You

belong

to

those

who

know

you . . .

vulnerable.

ON WHAT SIDE OF
THE CAGE **IS FREEDOM?**

Although there is a huge commotion about these behaviors, considered the evils of modern times, this type of reaction has always existed; the difference is that now it happens in a hyperconnected world, where we are constantly available and overwhelmed. In the past, cutting off long-distance communication was quite easy: You just stopped responding to letters, which in turn took months to arrive. Now that there are dozens of ways to reconnect, it's still a painful event, but with greater exposure.

Not responding to a person is proof that you're struggling to express your emotions, and it's also a betrayal of the responsibility you assume when you begin a relationship of any kind.

A person who disappears proves that they're not open to having an honest conversation about their decisions. With the excuse that disappearing hurts the other person less than confronting them, what they're really doing is getting rid of the bad feeling of having to take responsibility for their decision. These cases only prove that person's refusal to reach a higher emotional level or to recognize that future commitments, such as starting a business or a new relationship, will depend on more concrete actions, making pacts the phantom will not be willing to undertake.

They do it because they feel that it's a better alternative than showing their faces. Under the guise that this way they won't hurt the person they're ghosting, they leave the ghosted with an endless sense of sorrow because phantoms can be everywhere and appear when you least expect them. Ghosts haunt you incessantly. They keep you awake at night, worrying that you might run into them, yet they still haunt you while you sleep.

An increasing number of people are suffering from mental disorders after being subjected to this type of emotional punishment, which is an endless torture because instead of executing the victim, the executioner hides among memories and possibilities. Beyond the specific wound of loss, the rejected person feels a deep sense of abandonment that takes its toll on their self-esteem. Not knowing the causes of a breakup will make the person be more suspicious of the things they do, of how they behave, of being authentic. On the other hand, there will be a sense of not even deserving an answer, a feeling of inadequacy and disregard.

I'm addressing this topic here because there are already too many cases of people who have been subjected to this form of contempt, and many of them stop their progress. If this is your case, don't let the cowardice of others silence your roar.

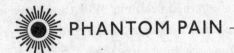 PHANTOM PAIN

Ghosting shows a total lack of empathy because it stems from a culture that sees reality as a video game that can be turned off when the game goes sideways, and you can avoid defeat with the restart button. In addition to a lack of empathy, these actions demonstrate emotional immaturity issues and a poor ability to identify one's own feelings, which are easier to abandon.

NOT EVERYONE DESERVES THE PRIVILEGE
OF BEING MISSED BY YOU.

To avoid having to go through the discomfort of telling a person, face to face or through virtual means, that they've decided to end the bond they have, they disappear, like spoiled and cruel children who flip the board if the game isn't going their way. In a move that has been widely criticized on social media, a Philippine congressman filed a bill to make ghosting punishable as an "offense that causes a sense of rejection and abandonment." Although I sympathize, I can't imagine how such a law could be enforced. I think it's only possible to eradicate these practices if we learn to have relationships based on empathy. This goes beyond feeling the pain of others; it's also the understanding that other people have an identity and feelings that are different from our own.

Those who suffer from being ghosted tirelessly go over each word and each event searching for a reason that in most cases doesn't exist. It's a continuous suffocation, a cycle that never ends, an open wound that is not allowed to heal. Although it can happen in any type of friendship, family, or work relationship, it is particularly complex in the case of romantic ones because it denies the rejected person a closure that would allow them to freely begin again. What's more, these wounds affect the future perception of how to approach love.

Failure to overcome ghosting can have consequences when approaching any new opportunity. You'll be afraid of making the same mistakes, without knowing what they were. Don't worry, getting out of this type of situation is possible, and I'm going to give you a series of actions that you can put into practice. First, take care of your inner dialogue. Go back to the self-awareness exercises earlier in the book. Keep in mind that what the other person did is entirely about them, not you. It's a problem rooted in their wounds and insecurities. Avoid trying to find the reasons in your actions, in your omissions. Don't fall into a mortifying evaluation of things that did or did not happen. While you may have made mistakes, none of them justify the other person's actions.

I WILL LOVE MYSELF
FOR THE LONG TERM.

Tell that being crying within you, "They decided to leave." "They didn't have the courage to talk to me." But never accuse yourself with an "I failed" or an "I scared them off." If this is the way you speak to yourself, note that these aren't phrases that come out of nowhere. You must ask yourself what's causing you to express yourself in this way. Do you feel you can't be loved? Do you think it wasn't worth it to stay by your side?

If your wounds of abandonment and rejection are still alive, encouraging your feelings of contempt, it's time to work on them to heal them once and for all.

Then you must follow this with another fundamental action: closing the cycle on your own. Don't look for this person to "put an end" to the situation, because that encounter can become an excuse to reestablish contact. Putting an end to it is something you must do alone, as decided by the person who couldn't show their face. Did you close the door but still hold the doorknob in your hand? When you close a circle, check to make sure you're not within the circumference.

Avoid anger. You may feel sadness, but it can turn into a persistent anger that can reflect on you, on what you feel. So deactivate the triggers that make you succumb to remembering and connecting with those feelings that caused you pain. You may think that deleting their accounts from your social media is as childish an action as the one that person has taken, but minimizing notifications, hiding and limiting their posts, if they haven't blocked you, will reduce the triggers to think about it all again.

Also, be prepared for their return. You should know how to

react when the person reappears, because they probably will. These reappearances, often referred to as *zombieing* (from zombie, a dead person who suddenly comes to life for strange reasons), can occur through direct contact or with approaches through social media or other digital media. It's essential that you prepare for their return. You must know what to do when this happens. If your decision is to talk to them, come up with a script of what you're going to say and follow it rigorously. This will make it easier to forgive and make the moment more bearable.

Put yourself first. That action sums up all the rest. You don't need anyone in order to pursue what you want, or for your life to have value. As we've seen in this book, even in the most complex situations you can find a way to get back to who you were before that wound.

Finally, talk to people you trust. Don't keep that pain inside or pretend that you're fine or that the situation doesn't affect you when the opposite is true. If you feel that you've reached a point where the damage is overwhelming, seek professional help. It's so normal to have an "I don't care" or "I'm fine and strong" reaction when it's not true. Doing this goes against the previous point's principle because you're putting yourself last, you're proving something that's not true, and believe it or not, that only sinks you deeper. Do the things you like, but do them for yourself, not because you want someone else to see them.

THE "SEE YOU SOON"
IS ALWAYS LATE.

And if you're the one playing the ghosting game, I ask you to think twice. You may have valid reasons for ending a relationship, but if you've come to this decision unilaterally, you need to let the other person know so that you can end the situation responsibly. Remember that no matter how disappointed you are, everyone deserves to know there's an end. Roaring also means taking responsibility, no matter how difficult that may be. If you're going to become part of someone's past, do so without becoming an unreal future.

 ## STIGMA

Strong and great are those who, knowing that they can hurt you, choose not to. The more love you put in your heart, the more room there is in it. Love doesn't fill the heart, it enlarges it; but it's also easier to give to those who have expanded hearts because they have more room.

So don't spend your time on something as petty as hatred. Hate doesn't create, it only destroys, but faith and hope will always win. I already said it in *Inquebrantables*: "Above those who run are those who fly and above those who fly are those who heal broken wings." Love so much and so extensively that you have no time or space left to hate anyone.

By all means, seek to eliminate and deactivate hatred from your life. If you continue in that vicious circle, you'll create a hole in your soul that is impossible to fill. You'll see an empty world without realizing that what you're looking at is merely a reflection of what you carry within you. Let's return to the theme of coming back to you, of not turning moments of grief into a show where you say that you're fine when it's not true. As I write these lines, there's a popular challenge on social media that invites people to show "a photo where you were devastated and no one knew it." I've seen

IF THEY
WANT
TO
LEAVE,
MAKE IT
EASY FOR
THEM.

dozens of posts with this title and I've discovered smiles, parties, scenes of immense joy. I myself see some of my photos, and it hurts to accept that many of them have a cry that is not heard, but that calls out, "Can you see me?" "Do you love me?"

These expressions, which few people can identify, are the ultimate portrait of one of today's most serious ailments: suicide.

When will we destigmatize suicide? Absurd prejudices end up discouraging a person from seeking help and then the worst happens: They don't get the timely intervention or follow-up they clearly need, and chaos ensues. We must erase this mark. We need to name suicide so that it is seen, so that it is clearly intervened in. It's essential that we all talk about this issue, and that we do so responsibly, carefully, respectfully, wisely, and from all sides, to find ways to prevent it. Let's act in time. If you want to help, go ahead and share, talk, detect, support, ask for help, go to therapy, do not be ashamed, stay informed, intervene, create awareness with your children, with your partner, with your friends. Stop judging, criticizing, and calling weak those who are experiencing depression, sadness, and don't know how to weather the storm like you, because suicide isn't about being brave or being a coward.

WORDS ENVY WHAT ACTIONS CAN SAY WHEN THEY'RE SILENT.

An act of love, of empathy, can save a life. So open your eyes and take a compassionate look at the world and let's find a way to get involved in this ever-growing problem.

According to the World Health Organization, seven hundred thousand people worldwide take their own lives each year. This figure is increasing at a faster rate than population growth, and the latest available estimates come from before the pandemic, before the financial and social crisis exploded. In the time you've been reading these paragraphs, two people have ended their lives.

We have long been told that suicide is a disease exclusive to rich and powerful nations. This is a myth, because while it's true that the per capita incidence rate is slightly higher in the developed world, nearly four out of every five suicides occur in developing countries. Suicide is an increasingly voracious beast that has found too many shadows to hide in the patterns of life our society has been adopting. It invades us because we don't know how much suffering can lie behind a smiling face.

Millions of families have been bereaved by suicide. The horror doesn't end with the lives lost, it lingers in the pain of unsatisfied answers, in the injustice of blame, and in the echo of deaths that could've been avoided. Devastation also happens when it's a suicide attempt.

One of the worst things about suicide is that it causes the most harm to the most vulnerable. It is one of the leading causes of death among teenagers and young adults.

 ## THE VERDICT

That morning we decided to do the same thing for different reasons. At the same time, we deliberately headed to that point of no return. There's a microsecond when the pressure breaks you. You make the fatal decision. Endless thoughts and emotions cross your mind; the list becomes unreadable. You don't understand or can't find answers to stop you. Heart and mind are divided. You think about family issues, the taunting, the betrayal, the absence, the tears, everything feels overwhelming. This isn't planned with precision.

You try to get everything right, but deep down you want everything to go wrong, until you start to cross that red line. Something in you is screaming "Go on!" but the frustration, the sadness is too much. No matter how hard you try, nothing brings you joy anymore. You don't want to sleep another day because you know how hard it will be to wake up again. You know you're going to crash and you speed up. They say that before you die, you see your life flash before your eyes, but for you it was a life you no longer wanted to see.

I DIDN'T WALK AWAY, **YOU PUSHED ME**.

You would've liked to say goodbye, but no one who escapes bids farewell. Why do I know all of this? Because I also experienced it. I speak to you about suicide with complete authority because I've been there. Some of us lucky ones were stopped by someone's love, a love that redeems you, casts shame to the bottom of the sea, and eclipses the past. Others will have the courage to overcome themselves. They will try to forget what happened that day. It will be a burden they will have to release daily so that they don't condemn themselves. There are those who will wish they had never tried it—they will never be the same again.

Others will simply leave an unfinished goodbye, and their voices will never be heard again. They will leave behind endless questions and silence as the only answer.

We can prevent this. By giving love to those who suffer, we may be able to stop this from happening. It's like unexpected events in the economy or in politics, when experts talk about the precedents, and find several indications that these events were going to happen, albeit only after they did. Before that, no one had foreseen it.

Something similar happens with those who decide to take their own lives. After the fact, we usually begin to find what we think are clear signs of what was going to happen, leaving loved ones with an indelible mark of pain, responsibility, and guilt.

First of all, it's not true that this situation always happens after a long process of reflection. The final decision can come in a short amount of time, suddenly. But in cases where the idea has been floating around for some time, one of the elements that can set off alarms is a radical change in behavioral patterns, especially if there is anger, agitation, excessive anxiety, and inordinate tendencies toward extravagance.

Also pay attention to a person's vocabulary, especially when there are catastrophic thoughts, when the person expresses that they want to die or that they're a burden to the people they love. In the United States, you can call 988 to reach the Suicide and Crisis Lifeline.

With every suicide, a family stops hearing their child's laughter forever.

With every suicide, a couple is left incomplete.

With every suicide, children are orphaned.

With every suicide, a sensitive heart stops beating.

With every suicide, an eternal silence is born.

FORGET THE DAMAGE THEY CAUSED YOU, BUT NOT THE LESSON LEARNED.

Don't let your guard down. Be a tireless watchdog for those around you. Suicide pays visits where you least expect it. Where smiles bloom, someone will say they had no idea.

This may not be your main goal, but don't let depression tarnish the stage of your triumphs with pain. Honorable mention goes to everyone who, no matter how broken they were, didn't give up, even though life insisted on mistreating them. And to those who read me with pain in their hearts, I embrace you for every time you had to cry alone.

In front of a mirror, with your eyes fixed on your eyes, repeat to yourself, "I swear I will forgive you, take care of you, bless you, help you, and love you every day of my life." I, too, hear voices inside me shouting "You can't!" but I make sure to crush them with God's promises. This is not your full stop. Don't believe just that you'll get it all back twofold, but that you'll also live to enjoy, share, and multiply it.

Take it slow. One day at a time. Today, rest from your fears, sorrows, secrets, and grudges. Fix yourself from within, straighten yourself out. Rest, relax those shoulders! Did you not realize how much tension you carry? Breathe . . . breathe again, but now with the awareness that you're filling yourself with life.

It doesn't matter where you think Jesus is, because wherever He is, a single word from Him will be enough to heal everything. Make the call. When you walk with God you don't count the number of miles to go, you simply rejoice that He is in control.

 ## THE LAST CALL

We carry a storm inside; that's why sometimes our eyes rain and sometimes our gaze roars. Roar as if you were able to escape death, as if you had nothing left to lose and every step you took was the last one needed to arrive. Roar as if you already knew lost times and the loneliness of eternal silence, as if each word were the universe's creative breath. Roar as if you no longer cared, as if there were no more ways out than victory. Imagine the attitude of someone who has come back from the dead or whose greatest threat is no more shocking than a simple memory.

Think of Lazarus when he opened his eyes, when he wiped off his unctions, when he smiled at those who mourned him. Who would have silenced his voice and his desire to satisfy what he did not take with him to eternity? We are all like Lazarus, who comes back to life, because it has been granted to us. And the next one will be eternal.

How would you threaten Lazarus? Nothing could intimidate he who has risen from the dead, not because he crossed the border of the inconceivable, but because he received the warmth of eternal life; not because he was chosen for the return journey, but because he experienced the joy of knowing the greatness that awaited him in the infinite.

Why threaten Lazarus? It would be useless to try to break someone who, after four days in a tomb, has learned to appreciate the beauty of simplicity, to discover the correctness of the imperfect, to enjoy what is imperceptible to most. You couldn't take anything away from the one who no longer counts the days in hours but in moments.

Who would threaten Lazarus? No one should dare challenge the one who has let go of all his fears and ambitions, all his narrow-mindedness and vanities, the one who would refuse the gold of the pharaohs to feel his feet on the sands of Bethany. There is no warning that intimidates those who discover brilliance where others only see decadence.

When would you threaten Lazarus? He wouldn't have time to consider the dangers or measure the extent of the risks. His vital interests would be the tangible and the authentic. He wouldn't say, "This view again," he wouldn't complain about his modest vegetable garden, not out of conformity, but because he knows how useless it is to long for the new if you haven't yet found joy in what you have.

How much would you threaten Lazarus? There are no dimensions to coerce the one who has set his course in the direction his heart dictates, the one who pushed aside the flagstone guided by the call of Christ, the one who folded the sheets to tend a bed in his room. Nothing will frighten the one whose only fear is not to be able to return to the arms of the Father.

How would you threaten one who was with the Almighty?

Humans are the only creatures who know that sooner or later we will die; therefore, we not only think about how we are going to live, but above all, how we are going to die.

IN MY DEFENSE, I WILL SAY THAT
I DECIDED TO PUT CHRIST FIRST.

You and I are accompanied throughout our lives by the idea of death. Moreover, this is an imminent fact. Faced with the intuition of its arrival, each person identifies themself as a sigh, as a flicker that becomes a residue of the future. The sky remains, and we just happen. As a result, the brave go about their business living as soon as they're certain of their end.

In a poetic sense, life ends up being the art of managing death. Death deepens our singularity because, in the end, each person understands it as their own. It is just about me. I'm the one death calls by name. I'm the one it targets without giving it the chance to pass as a friend. There is no escape; the deadlines are over. There is no more "I'll do it tomorrow," and no matter how hard

I try, pretexts will be of no use to me. That is why, by virtue of death, my existence is finally truly mine. Death is an intimate fact, it's a fascinating event, it's an experience that can't be transmitted to another. No one can teach you how to die, no one can die for someone else. And even if we could sacrifice ourselves for another, we wouldn't succeed in freeing them from their own death. For some it's a private tragedy; for others, a birthday in glory. Death is an ecumenical event, which comes to us all. It doesn't check ranks, portfolios, colors, or intellects. No one can escape from its arms. Whoever claims not to fear death, may not feel love either.

Our species still hopes to escape its death for one more day. It wishes with its soul to postpone it, pushing its faith to the limit. The last call doesn't allow for companions. That is why the question is: "How will death find you?" One can wait to die while surviving or one can live intensely while it makes itself known.

Even those of us who believe in eternal life are afraid of the transition it implies. Today more than ever, my conviction for heaven is real. I'm sure that this beautiful place where everything makes sense exists. Holding on to that certainty makes us vulnerable, but it also allows us to freely recognize that there's something better than life on this planet.

Let's love each other more so that we never regret using the time we have left in anger, resentment, or sadness. Let us not be foolish with the opportunity we have today. The last call is inevitable; the question is whether it will find us running and fleeing at the end or whether we will receive it in peace, knowing that we gave it our all.

How will you answer that last call? The best way is by loving with all your might, with all your mind, with all your soul. Simply by living. Even if sometimes we feel broken.

JUST TELL ME YOU **LOVE** YOURSELF.

HOW MUCH COURAGE DOES IT TAKE
TO SHOW UP UNARMORED?

Understanding death implies that we know how to value life. That is why we enjoy it with the intensity of someone who never forgets how the grains of sand fall and who roars before there is nothing left but the testimony of what they left unfinished.

Living with intensity is the greatest tribute we pay to those who left behind a list of dreams without checking them off, journeys that ended when they opened their eyes, concerts the size of their showers.

Roar now—time is running out.

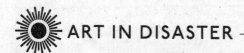 ART IN DISASTER

The shogun Ashikaga Yoshimasa didn't know he was about to find art the day a piece of his favorite tea set fell on the floor and burst into pieces. A disaster. The regent asked his servants to carefully pick up the pieces and send them to China for repair—that's where the artists who best knew how to work this material were located.

The shogun waited anxiously during the days it took for the piece to cross the East Sea and back—which must have been many considering the means of transportation five hundred years ago—but the end of the long wait was disappointing. When the order arrived, Yoshimasa found that his beloved cup, although it could once again hold boiling liquids without spilling them, had been put together in a sloppy manner and with ordinary materials. They had ruined the delicate beauty of the porcelain.

Outraged by the mediocrity, he asked the best craftsmen in his region to come to his aid. Pleased to be of service to the shogun, they set out to repair the broken piece with a refined technique that would maintain some of its original elegance. The potters searched for solutions until they came up with a mixture of resin and gold. Joined by this compound, the pieces of the cup not only retained their functionality but became even more beautiful than before they were broken. This technique that helps restore what is broken and gives renewed beauty to that which it repairs is called *kintsugi*—a fusion of the Japanese words for "gold" and "union"—and has become used for anything that elevates what has been damaged.

And so, the most beautiful faces are those that have accumulated great sorrow, but then regained their light because they never fell in love with the darkness. Just as skilled Japanese artisans learned how to make gems from pieces of pottery that were once considered garbage, you can rebuild that fractured heart, which you have long considered useless, with an infallible recipe: love.

Your life can be like a piece of *kintsugi*: a rearrangement of the fragments you are shedding in the arduous privilege of living. It can become more beautiful than it was when someone threw you to the ground and you were no longer one but a thousand pieces.

But that beauty is something you must learn to see. The shogun might well have discarded the cup amalgamated with gold dust if he hadn't already understood the power of beauty in simplicity, typical of Zen thinking, which facilitates the possibility of seeing that beauty in everyday things.

THERE ARE PEOPLE WHO DON'T EVEN DESERVE YOUR DISASTERS.

Wabi-sabi, an aesthetic trend that invites us to value the beauty hidden in the imperfect, the irregular, that which breaks with time, had flourished for centuries. Somehow things deteriorate, because nothing on earth is permanent. The scars of the soul, whether loose or joined by gold dust, are unmistakable signs of our humanity. Whoever can't love what is distorted and deteriorating ends up discarding self-love.

The great wonders of nature are nothing more than wounds of time; the sand of majestic beaches are rocks injured by the sea and the winds. We've simply educated our eyes to see it as something beautiful. We can always describe as beautiful that which we can't identify as such with the naked eye today. Sometimes, the beauty is hidden under the pain.

We can endure pain, resist it, and move on, as we've been taught. Tolerating the pressures of life is a lesson we've been learning and sharing for centuries, but no matter how much we're asked to resist, adversity can break or push us. The difference will be in our emotional preparation and in our ability to be resilient.

We refer to *resilience* as the ability we have to adapt to adverse situations, recover, and continue to grow stronger. I assume you've heard this term ad nauseam. I referred to it briefly earlier in this book, but I bring it up again because I feel it's essential to analyze all your attributes and needs so as to make the adjustments that will allow you to unleash your inner roar.

The concept of resilience isn't exclusive to psychology. It originally comes from physics, where it's used to describe the behavior of certain materials that have been impacted by external forces but are capable of recovering their original shape. This ability to regain an original shape is also studied in other disciplines, such as sociology, medicine, or epigenetics.

It became popular in the world of personal development through the contributions of Boris Cyrulnik, a renowned psychiatry and neurology researcher. The term has been used so much, and in so many contexts, that its original meaning has been obscured. Now a "resilient" person is most often seen as one who doesn't suffer, who overcomes problems, or who ignores their wounds when they fall. Similarly, it's associated with the ability to withstand the onslaught of life without experiencing change. But resilience can allow not only a return to normalcy, but also the development of better conditions than before the commotion.

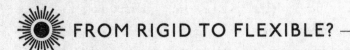 ## FROM RIGID TO FLEXIBLE?

The idea of resilience has been linked to attributes of tenacity, which makes us think of resilience as a prerequisite for a life of resignation. Strictly speaking, tenacity reflects the energy a material can withstand before it breaks, the resistance it exerts to avoid distortion. To draw an analogy with human realities, it would be the strength a person has to resist pressure, suffering, or exhaustion before breaking.

IF YOU'RE SAD, IT'S A GREAT TIME TO PAY CLOSE ATTENTION TO YOURSELF.

For example, we can jump on a glass table and, no matter how hard it is, eventually it will break because it has almost no ability to bend during a collision. On the other hand, resilience is like jumping on a trampoline, which receives energy and then returns it with an elastic prowess, because it has the ability to go back to its original shape.

If you're inflexible, you will break. Don't try to be invincible; focus on the ability to fiercely transform what is hurting you. It's not about

**When you
smile**
the sun
doesn't rise,
you set it.

erasing it; it's about intervening in it. We all have the beautiful virtue of transforming a lethal blow into something honorable. Resilience is just the power to articulate your biological, historic, emotional, and social strengths to change the reality in which you find yourself.

Although we've stolen these terms from the pure sciences, their meaning is amplified when we use them to explain the convulsions of the soul. They no longer focus on or refer to the pure and hard resistance of a material, or to its ample ability to lose and regain its shape. Instead, from the heart, the mind, and the soul, a virtuous triangle is created where the strategies are born that are used by someone like you or me to make a bitter situation not sterile.

Resilience is an intensive process, at once psychological, biological, and strategic. It is holistic. Your spirit, heart, and mind are united as an opposition of positive forces and tensions that make you who you are. Even if you don't have a significant percentage of harmony or balance, you still decide to live your life in an intense, passionate, intentional, provocative way, and, consequently, full of pleasant moments caused by a conviction that overcomes any emotion. Resilience sustains the present and forges the future, destroys the bonds of shame and the state of inadequacy, puts an end to the fatalistic idea that everything is over, turns a cry into a roar, and not that of someone who is wounded. Resilience is not an eraser, but the craftsman who manipulates the broken clay.

Jeremiah 4:19 exclaims, "My anguish, my anguish! I am pained at my very heart; my heart is disquieted in me; I cannot hold my peace; because thou hast heard, O my soul, the sound of the trumpet, the alarm of war."

We can only be resilient if we are able to accept and process negative emotions. Denying them won't give you the resilience to see them through. A material doesn't accumulate and expand energy that it doesn't receive. You don't just react to external stimuli; challenging yourself can stretch the supports that propel you from within.

Let's go again! Yesterday you fell, but tomorrow you will rise by the hand of Christ. That is the faith of resurrection, the power to turn a period into a comma along your way. To be resilient, to improve with every stumble, that is the right grammar of God. He doesn't leave us, He continues to reign and to hear our cry. This difficulty will not defeat you; it will elevate you. It will not break you; it will strengthen you. Not only will you stand up, but your footing will be stronger.

I AM LEARNING TO FAIL
MORE SUCCESSFULLY THAN BEFORE.

We've all been resilient to a greater or lesser extent. We were resilient when we smiled again after the slap of a betrayal blew our teeth out, when we dressed up for the first interview after being fired, when we dared to say yes, even though we carried the weight of an immense no. Even if you don't know it, you're already resilient, at least a little, and that natural ability can be strengthened.

The first and perhaps most important step is to make progress—as you've been doing—in your inner knowledge. Get to know your talents and tendencies, the biases of your decisions, and the power to control your desires. The second step is not to isolate yourself from emotions. Feeling what is happening and accepting that it affects us and hurts us is necessary for our sensitive material to withstand the shock and bounce back.

Embrace the pain and give it time to heal—you can't get rid of a sorrow you deny.

To act with resilience you must set out to return to God and realize that many things would have been closer to the ideal if you had acted differently. From the cradle we're drilled that we should never regret what we do. The motto of no regrets has given titles to books and songs because it contains an undeniable reality: We are the product of the accumulation of our actions. The idea sounds good but putting it into practice is a bit complex. Is there anything you regret? I'm sure there is, and often it's not about what you did wrong, it's about what you never did.

Inaction and the refusal to act are the heaviest burdens we carry. Of what remains unrealized, we are only left with hypotheses, fantasies, and the enormous burden of asking ourselves, "Why didn't I study what I wanted to?" "Why didn't I say what I meant?" "Why was I afraid to go there?"

Regret shouldn't anchor you to the past; it's a way to better understand a new future. Remorse binds us to the past, from which we get nothing of value. On the other hand, repenting isn't about thinking about what we did or did not do, but about starting the future by recognizing what was important, by knowing how to rethink what is appropriate.

Understanding which of our decisions was wrong leads us to reflect and consider a new reality. This process is only possible when an alternative future appears in our mind, and only by looking through it do we activate effective thinking.

Being resilient requires these reflections to make us more flexible, to give us a new drive to be better.

 RETURN TO GOD

There are many people I know who, when reflecting on a big mistake in their lives, regret having turned their backs on God and lived apart from Him. Although He calls us thousands of times in our lives, many complain that they never receive His call because they don't realize that in the purity of His heart is the harmony that connects with His voice. Only the affable hearts, who train their sensitivity and don't allow themselves to be callused by the evils of the world, will manage to hear that voice that leads them to His will. But those who carry an angry and barricaded heart hide in the cliffs of their prejudices and ignore the signs, calls, and instructions of the eternal.

THERE AREN'T ENOUGH SHOOTING STARS
FOR ALL MY WISHES.

Our great challenge is to stop being proud. One of the extreme sports humans engage in is keeping pride in check. Not watching over it means opening the door and letting it take over our daily lives. It's always tough when someone exposes our mistakes, calls us out for being mean, and brings up the wound we don't want to see. Therefore, if we're humble enough to recognize our mistakes, we can clean our emotional garbage, bring it into the light, and walk the path of bliss.

If you allow your heart to wither, you'll cease to feel, respond, and opt for a new direction and you'll continue on the same path you've already traveled all your life. The fossilized heart is embedded in unbelief and defiance of God, becomes insensitive to reprimand, and can no longer be moved to a new and better way of being. An insensitive heart loses its fear of getting hurt. This gives free rein to debauchery to take absolute control of our lives; it leads us to imprudence and recklessness, so we break other hearts without being aware of their emotions.

No one with a hard heart could be considered a hero. They are nothing more than a fool and, without exception, someone who will face circumstances that will break them, after they have mowed down those around them.

Do you want to know if you have a hardened heart? There are notable traits that can help you discover if your heart has begun to lose flexibility, if it has started going down the short path of turning to stone. Ask yourself:

- Have you begun to have more and more trouble accepting what God says?
- Do you reject His authority?
- Do you criticize everything you do not recognize in yourself?
- Do you show an attitude of indifference toward others and their pain?
- Do you justify your behavior?
- Does pride prevent you from apologizing?
- Do you resist being corrected and think you're always right?
- Do you begin to care more about goods and prestige than about love and goodness?
- Do you have little interest in spiritual matters?
- Do you act with total indifference to the affairs of family and friends?
- Do you reject the reading of wisdom texts, prayer, and supplication?

You are the one who can open the door of your life to the Lord. He will always be with you, no matter how difficult your situation may be. Do not try to solve everything; participate in His work without trying to change it. You will do what is possible, the rest is His favorite toy: the impossible.

Return to God. Do it today. Pray for your anger and let it crack the scabs of your soul. Let go of your stubbornness and run forward, where His grace is. Return to God. He is able to give life to a heart buried in bitterness and dead with anger. Everything He does is new. The surgery lasts a second—the recovery is up to you.

THE PLACE YOU LEFT AT GOD'S TABLE
IS STILL AVAILABLE.

If you are a believer—and if you are not—I recommend you pray. I've prepared this prayer for when you feel far away from Him:

Lord, forgive my wickedness, my lukewarmness. Forgive me for having let love become cold. Forgive those who with a hard heart have oppressed the weak and the poor.

I ask you to break the curses and uproot the hardness of my family line that has caused so much harm. Deliver me from the blindness of my soul, from the deafness of my heart, from stinginess and gossip. Protect me from deceit and traps. Dismantle the obstacles and straighten every bent back.

I give You every stubbornness that causes me to retreat. Give me a heart that conforms to Yours, and the wisdom to recognize the meaning of its weight. I ask You to give me kindness accompanied by resolve and contentment, a bright attitude of gratitude for my daily bread. And I humbly ask that You imbue me with the generosity of Your wisdom.

Give me fire in my spirit, passion, and a heart that burns for how Christ moves my life. Rekindle my faith so that I understand that the mystery of the supernatural is also for me.

Bless the air that I inhale and contain. Turn it into the roar of the facts that I will build with tireless effort, with inexhaustible courage, because I bathe it in faith.

THE REALM OF YOUR EXISTENCE

Let's talk about your silences, your laments at dawn, the lump in your throat and the pain in your neck from turning back so often, the stabbing in your chest, the trembling of your eyes, and the shaking of your hands. Yes, let's talk about all that struggle, the preparation that has allowed you to see the courage within you and the strength you have to endure these situations with such dignity. Come. Learn to see your wounds as signs of audacity.

You have already inhaled a breath of fresh air that filled your soul with the best of you and inflamed your lungs with the necessary tools to bring out your inner roar. The time has come to love yourself for the long haul, to love your quirks, to embrace yourself out loud, to judge yourself with compassion for what you feel, to go out at night to collect stars, and to reassess your priorities. Love is a decision and the miracle is choosing it every day. Love yourself the way God has shown you is possible. It's wonderful when things don't go as planned but turn out the way you needed them to.

The bad days are behind you. Now you can start creating your magnificent life. It is a choice. You can either let yourself be carried away by your tendencies or emphasize the spiritual. You will be faced with determining where to find value and how to create your essential hierarchies. You can put your weight on the symbol bearers, on the idols of immediacy, on the butchers who will choose your ribs as the next piece to be displayed in the hunger bazaar. You can ride on the stock market seesaw, on the unraveling fashion carousel, on the red carpets of the abyss.

The heart has no limits, and the mind doesn't understand that. You can raise portraits of auburn-headed or bearded despots, of those with gelled hair or spotless kepis. You can recite complete passages from the manuals of hatred or sing at the top of your lungs the hymn of the ghosts that sow misery. You will surrender to the rise and fall of empty sex, wake up next to names that were never shared with you, blur the screens that reflect frustrations. You will know how to hang yourself with the vanity of silk or lift your body with iron clamps. Those will be your choices.

Pride is an evil that arises from refusing to accept the power of God and His love, while He reveals your mistakes through a friend, an adversary, a spouse, a mother, or a stranger whom you know to be right. Therefore, we must improve our attitudes and correct our mistakes, since pride leads us to "counterattack" and immediately point out the defects of the one who questions us, uselessly seeking to refute and minimize the importance of their message instead of accepting the criticism or correction. We must apologize and strive to be better.

You flee from the truth and return with an anger that oozes from your wound, with a fury that comes from suspicion. You shelter yourself with the icy feeling of inadequacy that comes from ignoring love.

Pride pushes you to fury, to vengefulness, to the attack that robs you of the opportunity to improve. It deprives you of seeing miracles and the obvious signs of the supernatural. It has such an effect that it blinds you and doesn't allow you to see beyond your limited personal prejudices, which demonstrate your distorted and lacking vision of life. At times, the pride that invades you is so great that it drives people away from you, making you undesirable. Despite this, you have been given a hundred opportunities to change, to improve your attitude, to live in humility, and to mend your mistakes. Pride is an obstacle, a wall between the blessing and the curse.

God's love is very powerful, but He will act as much as you allow Him to do so. God never forces you to accept Him because He will never override your freedom. Of course He wants you to receive Him in all areas of your existence, but He will never annul your freedom. Let Him in so that He can cleanse you of everything that separates you from a better life.

Once the time comes to roar, ask yourself who runs the realm of your existence, where are the patterns that command your values. God can be the center of all hierarchy, even when you don't believe in Him, because if you build your life honoring what is important and beautiful, delicate and sensitive, you will have put God on the first altar of your honor, even if you don't know it.

May He be your starting point and your destination, and may you never stop moving forward.

Although it may sound extremely difficult, keep going. You have inhaled enough air in reflection and self-awareness, you have held it in long enough while you focused and reframed your decision biases. You know that you can only release your cry with your willpower and the direction of your purpose, and even if you've been shattered to pieces, the union of your fragments will turn your simplicity into a fine jewel.

Truth is not a tourist destination.

From the outside, we don't know when the volcano will erupt, but you are inside, containing the heat. Let your chest feed the detonation of your throat, and let your ideas fuel your heart. Ignite, until you reach the point of reaction.

Inhale, inflame, and roar.

The time has come for you to be heard.

Roar, or Expect to Be Devoured!

LOVE!

It's later than you think.

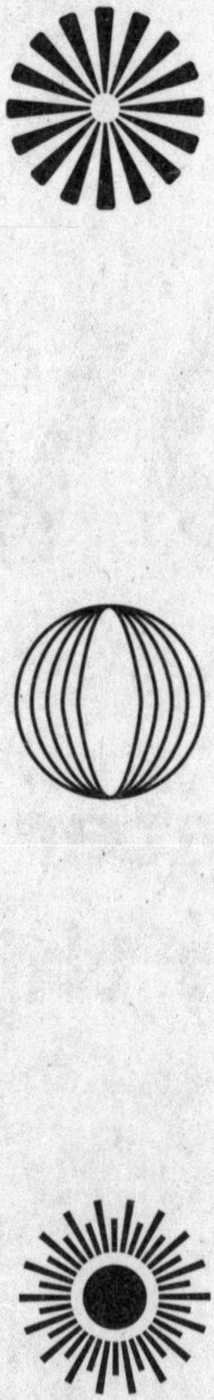

Epilogue

To live better, we must not hold on, we must let go. We must live without retaining, without clinging. Let's live without obsessing over time. Let's stop counting the seconds, and by living, let's lose the notion that they exist.

Let's detach ourselves and integrate ourselves into the whole. Let's accept how small we are, but how much we are worth in this universe. We must wait for nothing and everything, without attachment; simply wait and, in the waiting, discover ourselves in the mystery and let the hows surprise us. Let's do so knowing that not everything that happens to us is good, but it's necessary. Sometimes God takes some people from us for our protection and leaves others for our learning. If some leave, let them go; if some stay, let them be.

I ask Christ to deliver you from blindness of the soul, from obsession with speed and deafness of heart, from stinginess and gossip. I ask Him to protect you from deceit, from the traps of others and from your own mind. I ask Christ that you begin to dismantle all the obstacles that hold you back. I ask Him to straighten your back bent by the weight of life.

Today, wherever you may be reading this text, give Him every foolishness of the heart: "I give it to you, Lord." Surrender to Him every pride that makes you turn back and keeps you away from those you love and from those you are loved by. Ask Christ for a heart like His own, but above all, ask Him to give you the wisdom to understand the weight and the implications of having such a big heart. I want you to be filled with kindness, accompanied by firmness, joy, and a bright attitude of gratitude for your daily bread.

After going through these pages together, after what I've said to you and what you've reflected on, I hope that you're filled with a longing worth pursuing and that you may humbly be imbued with virtue and with every gift of the eternal. In this moment, may God give you the fire of the spirit and an unwavering heart that is ready to burn for the movement of our Father's things.

Nothing can threaten you anymore because you are the child of everything. Those who roar know that they will never be devoured. Roar!

I hope that after reading this book
**you will love yourself completely,
and not in pieces.**

Notes

Step One: INHALE

1. Howard Gardner, *Frames of Mind: The Theory of Multiple Intelligences* (New York: Basic Books, 2011).
2. Lise Bourbeau, *Heal Your Wounds and Find Your True Self* (Quebec: Editions E.T.C. Inc., 2020).
3. Lise Bourbeau, *Heal Your Wounds and Find Your True Self* (Quebec: Editions E.T.C. Inc., 2020).

Step Two: INFLAME

1. S. Vosoughi, D. Roy, and S. Aral, "The Spread of True and False News Online." *Science* 359, no. 6380 (2018): 1146–1151.
2. Francesco Cirillo, *The Pomodoro Technique* (New York: Crown Currency, 2018).
3. CNBC, "Jeff Bezos at the Economic Club in Washington," Milestone Celebration Dinner at the Economic Club in Washington in Washington, DC, September 13, 2018, YouTube video, https://www.youtube.com/watch?v=xv_vkA0jsyo .
4. Solomon E. Asch, "Studies of independence and conformity: I. A minority of one against a unanimous majority," *Psychological Monographs: General and Applied* 70 (1956): 1–70.
5. Robert B. Cialdini, *Influence: The Psychology of Persuasion* (New York: HarperBusiness, 2021).

Step Three: ROAR

1. Walter Mischel, *The Marshmallow Test: Understanding Self-Control and How to Master It* (New York: Bantam Press, 2014).
2. Marc Winn, "What Is Your Ikigai?" *The View Inside Me* (blog), May 14, 2014, https://theviewinside.me/what-is-your-ikigai/.
3. Mike Michalowicz, *Profit First: Transform Your Business from a Cash-Eating Monster to a Money-Making Machine* (New York: Portfolio, 2017).

About the Author

DANIEL HABIF is considered one of the best and most recognized Spanish-speaking motivational speakers and authors in the world. He's collectively sold more one million copies of his Spanish language bestsellers: *Inquebrantables, Las Trampas Del Miedo*, and *Ruge*. He's appeared at hundreds of international conferences, selling more than 700,000 tickets and performing in 170 cities in 25 different countries around the world. A longtime advocate for human rights, he's shared the stage with presidents, governors, Nobel Prize winners, and international leaders working for change. Visit him at www.danielhabif.com.